Date Due

THE RIDDLE OF VIOLENCE

Kenneth Kaunda

THE RIDDLE
OF
VIOLENCE

Edited by

Colin M. Morris

1817

HARPER & ROW, PUBLISHERS, SAN FRANCISCO
Cambridge, Hagerstown, Philadelphia, New York
London, Mexico City, São Paulo, Sydney

FIRST U.S. EDITION

Library of Congress Cataloging in Publication Data

Kaunda, Kenneth David, Pres. Zambia, 1924-
   The riddle of violence.

   First published in 1980 under title: Kaunda on violence.
   1. Violence — Zambia.   2. Nonviolence.
I. Morris, Colin M.   II. Title.
HN803.Z9V54 1981   303.6′2′096894   80-8348
ISBN 0-06-250450-9

81 82 83 84 85 10 9 8 7 6 5 4 3 2 1

Contents

Preface

This book has been a long time arriving. It was promised months before it was finally delivered, but the problems of Southern Africa have occupied me to the exclusion of everything else.

My grateful thanks go to my good friend and fellow freedom fighter, Dr Colin Morris, who edited the manuscript. For fifteen years whilst he lived in Zambia we worked closely together, and since he has been based in London, he has made frequent trips out to Zambia so that we might continue our long collaboration. We have talked, argued and agonized over this matter of violence together since 1958 when we first met – I, a freedom fighter under restriction in Kabompo; he, a young missionary, already making a name for himself on the Copperbelt as an outspoken champion of human rights.

Colin Morris and I have long shared common ground because we believe in the same principles insofar as the rights of man are concerned, and we are at one in our obedience to God our Father. I am proud that I can count him as a comrade in our common struggle, as a literary collaborator and most of all as a personal friend. He has done much to clarify my thinking, challenge my assumptions and direct my attention to books and articles and ideas I had not come across. One book in particular to which he drew my attention I have found most helpful – Professor Michael

Walzer's *Just and Unjust Wars*, (Basic Books, New York, 1978). I gladly acknowledge my debt to Professor Walzer's ideas.

I must also mention gratefully my publisher Lady Collins, who patiently but firmly urged me on to finish the manuscript. I did not do too well this time, but promise her I will try harder next time! My Personal Secretary, Mrs Gloria Sleep has for years transcribed my hastily scribbled thoughts and so provided the raw material of this book.

This book would have been just a theoretical treatise if it had not been for the Zimbabweans, young and old, who sacrificed so much for the cause. I also acknowledge the devotion of citizens of the Front Line states, especially Zambia, who have given their lives in the cause of human dignity and freedom.

Finally, I must not forget to thank my long-suffering family whose inexhaustible patience has made it possible for me to write this book. Without their unfailing support there is little I could do.

KENNETH DAVID KAUNDA
President of the Republic of Zambia

State House
Lusaka
24 April 1980

Introduction

So far as I know, President Kaunda keeps no private diary. Instead he sets down his thoughts about virtually anything of more than ephemeral interest which occupies his mind during the course of the day. His personal secretary transcribes these notes on to distinctive blue paper. These form an important record of the thought-processes of a statesman, though that is not the primary intention – which is simply to retain for further reflection a few of the great stream of concerns which flow through his working life. An average 'blue paper' might include some trenchant comments about the words or deeds of some other world statesman as reported in that morning's BBC World Service news bulletin, one or two attempts at some verses of poetry, a passage from the Bible or some other book he has been reading and, at greater length, the first draft of a speech to be made or a policy statement to be issued to the press.

From time to time he has asked me to abstract all the passages which deal with a given subject he wants to consider in more depth or else offer to a wider public for debate. This is how two previous books came to be written – *A Humanist in Africa* (Longmans 1966) and *Letter to My Children* (Longmans 1973). Once I have selected the raw material, we then explore it together, my job being to get him to explain the bits I find obscure, enigmatic or plainly at odds with other bits. I then go away and produce a draft which is based upon our discussion of his text. This he works on, expanding this, altering that or sometimes scrapping the lot. But by the end it says what he wants to say, and a series of unconnected passages written down over a period of time come together to form a theme. We have kept this running collaboration going for over twenty years – since the publication of *Black Government?* USLL in 1960 at the height of the freedom struggle in Northern Rhodesia which was to lead to Kenneth David Kaunda's election as first President of an independent Zambia.

Since 1965 until a few weeks ago, President Kaunda has been preoccupied, almost to the point of obsession, with Rhodesian UDI* and its effects not only upon Zambia but the whole of Southern Africa. Those blue Cabinet papers are a fragmentary but moving private history of the tragedy. Noted are the plans which came to nothing, the diplomatic initiatives which failed – the anxious search for any alternative to an escalating war. Then as the peacemakers ran out of time, there are the President's reactions to the blood letting, the bombing raids on Zambia, the crushing effect on Zambia of economic sanctions aimed at Rhodesia. His dealings with the guerrilla leaders, disputes with Britain and parleyings with South Africa are all noted. All these elements, and more, in the fifteen-year crisis are recorded in the blue papers, not as a continuous narrative but in cryptic comments and scribbled down thoughts. Undoubtedly, when President Kaunda's account of the UDI years is published it will have a unique authority for he and Mr Smith alone share the distinction of having had starring roles in the drama from the first day to

*Unilateral Declaration of Independence

10

the last, whereas British Prime Ministers and Foreign Secretaries have come and gone, four US presidencies have run their course and South Africa has had three Prime Ministers during that time.

This book is not that firsthand account of UDI, though it is obvious that President Kaunda's convictions about violence have been fundamentally affected by the freedom struggle in Southern Africa. I was asked to include only such references to the UDI issue as would make the argument intelligible and provide illustrations of the main theme. Without doubt, President Kaunda was stung by the volume of criticism he attracted because of his support for the freedom movements in Zimbabwe and Namibia, especially protests coming from religious quarters. He had been the darling of the pacifist cause – possibly the only world leader since Gandhi to preach and practise non-violence from a position of power. His change of mind and heart was seen more as an act of apostasy than one of those convenient U turns politicians make from time to time to get their policies back in line with reality.

Many pacifists will remain unconvinced by President Kaunda's arguments. For them there can be no compromise on the issue of violence – it is an unmitigated evil and they will have no truck with it. Nor have Dr Kaunda's views, set down in the material I have examined, evolved in such a way as to make a systematic defence easy. This is not how it is in real life. Only from some university lecture rooms and pulpits do thoughts on grave moral issues emerge as clean-cut propositions marching irresistibly to neat and unambiguous conclusions. The nearer you get to the cockpit of action and the more complex the issue to which you must respond with hard decisions, the more the moral imperatives dissolve into dilemmas.

UDI, it should be remembered, was a crisis of the utmost legal, constitutional, political and military complexity, and it dragged on for fifteen years. Is it possible to be at the very heart of a maelstrom for all that time without your views on such a highly contentious issue as violence undergoing some modification? Can you, in time of war, hold life or death power over millions of people without engaging in a constant exercise in self-questioning and inner anguish? That is what this essay records. It is not a defence but an explanation of how a statesman had to make up his mind on the question which makes cowards of us all – can I reconcile love for my neighbour with using violence against him; on the other hand, can I stand by whilst my neighbour uses violence against *his* neighbour? Most reasonable people will probably answer No to each half of that question, and find themselves impaled on the horns of a dilemma. The pain is all the greater if you happen to be a national leader who cannot just decide for himself what he should do but must also impose decisions on all his people. That sort of pain is more like crucifixion and I believe some of the anguish will be felt by any sensitive reader.

I have not found it easy to contain the subject within reasonable bounds. Dr Kaunda writes easily and at length across a very wide canvas and moves between the fields of politics, philosophy and theology without any sense of having crossed a frontier. The essay itself was written during a period of roughly eighteen months; more precisely, he began it at the end of 1978, then there was a gap of almost a year when the President was too busy coping with the problem of escalating violence in Southern Africa to be able to spare time to write about it. He put the finishing touches to the manuscript on his return from the Zimbabwe independence celebrations in April 1980, during a three-day spell in hospital for a medical check-up.

I have taken some liberties with syntax in order to make for a smoother narrative and also removed a few personal references, mostly Dr Kaunda's responses to my comments, which though precious to me are of no interest to the reader. I was greatly helped by a recently published work by two former members of the University of Zambia – *Zambia Foreign Policy: Studies in Diplomacy and Dependence*, Douglas G. Anglin and Timothy M. Shaw, Westview, 1979. The meticulous scholarship of these two old friends saved me some of the labour of checking dates, places and events.

I am very much indebted to Mrs Gloria Sleep, Dr Kaunda's personal secretary, who guided me through the blue papers and to Miss Jean Palk who typed several drafts of the manuscript.

COLIN M. MORRIS

PART ONE

Light from the East

I was first introduced in a serious way to the ideas of
Gandhi by Rambhai Patel, a Lusaka store keeper, who
made rough and ready translations of some of the
Mahatma's writings, especially passages from his life story.
I in turn fed these ideas into my earliest political speeches
where, it seems to me now, they shone like gems in a river
of mud. It was a noble gesture on Rambhai's part. I was
penniless at the time, trying to make my way in politics and
support a young family, so food came before books and the
fighting fund of Congress before either.

Of course my friend Patel has always insisted that the
help he gave me was an investment in Zambia's future. He
thought it wise to try to spot winners amongst the young
hopefuls jostling one another near the top of the heap in the
infant nationalist movement. He might even say it was an
act of self-preservation for if, as seemed likely, Central
Africa was to go up in flames, he was one of those with
most to lose – so he saw to it that the case for non-violence,
Gandhi's doctrine of *satyagraha*, was firmly implanted in
the minds of those he guessed might be future leaders. It
was Rambhai's joke – for all his sardonic humour he was a
deadly serious disciple of Mahatma Gandhi. He paid the
bills when in 1958, as Secretary General of Congress and on
the point of taking over its leadership, I visited India,

making a pilgrimage to some of the places associated with Gandhi's life and work. I owe Rambhai Patel much and can see why Jesus made a shrewd businessman the hero of one of his parables of the Kingdom.

Gandhi's philosophy deepened and broadened my own thinking which had been based on a rather narrow but enthusiastic mission-station Christianity. The Gospel preached by the Reverend Robert McMinn, who was missionary in charge at Lubwa during my childhood and early youth, was Bible-centred to the letter, evangelical in tone and sternly moral to the point of harshness. For all its sincerity and passion, it was not easily translated into political terms. But then, the old man believed he was preparing generations of African young people to be citizens of heaven from which the sordid goings-on of politics are banished. Some of his students had different ideas. Looking back, I can see that even in the late afternoon of the colonial day, it took a very far-sighted missionary to imagine a near future in which Africans ruled modern nations throughout the continent, let alone agree that the Christian gospel could be the accelerator of a political engine and not its brake.

If I owe my faith to Jesus, Mahatma Gandhi supplied the hope. His teachings flooded my mind with light, brightening those dark corners where I stored perplexing questions I had gnawed on for years without result. For instance: how is it possible for a Christian to be an effective politician *without hurting anyone*? Obviously, the politician who does not have to take seriously the commandment to love his neighbour as himself can plough ahead remorselessly, accepting as the price of efficiency the casualties strewn along the way. On the other hand the politician who is a Christian might easily carry compassion to the point of soft-headedness, doing harm by his weakness rather than through cruelty.

These and such like grave questions preoccupied my youthful mind as I got deeper into politics and realized how often the politician must do hard things and make decisions for which he will not be loved and may even be hated. I fear I was a very intense young man and sometimes made a fool of myself as I struggled to give birth to thoughts too profound for my experience. Looking back I see no need to apologize for that formality of speech which must sometimes have sounded pompous for I and my companions had hold I think of the right questions. We were the victims of a violent society – a violence no less terrible because it was dressed up in the splendid uniforms of imperialism; a colour bar no less cruel because it was usually applied with kindness; laws no less repressive because they were administered with scrupulous fairness.

The underdog in such a society who goes into politics, especially if fate makes him a leader, cannot avoid facing up to the issue of violence – the use of force against injustice. And if such a one is a Christian, as I was, then the torment is terrible. Can I, in the very act of striking him, love my neighbour who happens to be wearing a police or army uniform? Should a Christian leader urge his followers to take part in campaigns of disobedience and civil disruption which, in a tense society where racial feeling is running high, could well lead to violence?

In those final days of colonialism, events seemed to move at a terrifying speed towards some end – disaster or triumph who could tell? Much of the force that hurried things along came, of course, from Africa to the north of us where tens of millions of our brothers and sisters had won their freedom and were urging us on. It was the thunder of their dancing feet we heard in our ears – a sound as welcome to us as it was doomful to the white colonialists. But at no point in the sweep of events could we ask for a respite to think. It was like negotiating the Zambezi in flood – only the next rock and obstacle counted – there was no breathing space in which to plot a long-term course. To someone like myself in such straits, buffeted by events, inwardly torn by moral dilemmas, Gandhi's concept of *satyagraha*, the creative use of non-violent resistance as a strategy for change, was a lifebelt thrust into the hand of a drowning man.

The doctrine was all the more attractive because the personality of the teacher was so warm. Gandhi was my ideal. He had brought to perfection all the qualities I was struggling to develop – self-discipline, austerity, oneness with the people, holiness that was not stuffy – sanctity with a sense of humour – and practical wisdom. He understood what was in the heart of man. He could read men's souls and so knew how to exploit human weakness for good purposes. A free and independent India was the first and greatest of the nations of the so-called Third World. She was the Mecca or Jerusalem towards which weary freedom fighters on other continents turned for inspiration when things were going badly for them.

So it was according to the principles of non-violence on the Gandhi model that the final stages of the freedom struggle in Zambia were conducted. The doctrine became the official policy of the United National Independence Party* and apart from a few regrettable lapses, it was

---

* UNIP was the party founded by Dr Kaunda and others in 1959 after the banning of the short-lived ZANC.

honoured by the masses, whose discipline in the face of
grave provocation was remarkable. Almost as hard to bear
as the aggressive tactics of the police and army were the
sneers of our opponents who thought all the exhortations
to non-violence were at best hypocrisy and at worst
weakness. But had we acted on the basis of a blow for a
blow, the history of the last days of Northern Rhodesia and
the first days of Zambia would have been written in blood.

But it was another Indian, Kasterbhai Narayan who in
the early sixties long before the freedom struggle was over,
unwittingly sowed in my mind the seeds of some disquiet-
ing thoughts about non-violence. They have since ger-
minated to surplant the strong, simple concepts of classical
satyagraha with more ambiguous, complex and not
altogether satisfactory ideas. Not that Mr Narayan had any
doubts about the efficiency of *satyagraha*. He was in Dar es
Salaam as a member of the Reverend Michael Scott's International Peace Brigade – a task force of pacifists which
aimed to march south from Tanzania in order to liberate
Northern Rhodesia (as it then was) from the Central
African Federation using only the weaponry of the Spirit.
They would be armed solely with the sacred scripture of
whatever religion they avowed, go to prison in droves and
bring key centres of the country to a halt by lying or sitting
down in main roads and across railway tracks. Sir Roy
Welensky, the Federal Prime Minister, would then resign in
exasperation and hand the country over to its rightful
owners. That was the theory.

I fell to talking with Mr Narayan who was very pleased
to learn that I was a disciple of Mahatma Gandhi and committed to the doctrine of *satyagraha*. He seemed to feel,
however, that I was in danger of polluting the purity of my

pacifist vocation by getting mixed up in a nationalist movement whose aims were political. Just as Gandhi resigned from the Indian National Congress in 1936 and chose to go it alone, so Mr Narayan appealed to me to resign all political offices and take up the family trade – my father having been a travelling evangelist – and spread the gospel of *satyagraha* by preaching and example.

Kasterbhai Narayan is a man of great holiness and I have always believed that God sends holy men and women across our path with messages it is foolish to ignore. So I was thrown into great confusion and went through days of mental torment, questioning my motives for political leadership.

In the nicest possible way Mr Narayan was in effect accusing me of betraying my idol, Gandhi, for the fake but glittering prizes of political power. Whether he knew it or not, he had touched a most sensitive nerve. I had, and still have, mixed feelings about public office. One part of me, and a big part at that, shrinks from the necessary antics of the political circus, the lure of the publicity trap and the will to domination every leader must, however regretfully, develop. The temptation to become a wilderness saint, living on the Zambian equivalent of locusts and wild honey and refining my spirit by punishing my body, was very attractive to me.

At that time, the hard days of the freedom struggle still lay ahead, and if there was one thing I feared more than any suffering I might have to endure myself it was the possibility I should prove to be a false shepherd and lead my fellow countrymen to their doom. I could not see much light at the tunnel's end. And I did not need to be a prophet, only a student of the newspapers to guess that my immediate future must be taken up with still more strife, more imprisonment, more disruption of home and family life – more of everything, in fact, that had made my life almost unbearable.

After a couple of sleepless nights I decided that Mr Narayan was mistaken. Or at least. . . . if indeed he had brought a message from God for me, it must somehow have got jumbled up on the way. The people had asked me to lead them and I had taken them into the depths of a very dark and frightening wood. I did not see how I could abandon them, only to appear again as the servant of a higher destiny, urging them to try a more excellent way as they milled about in confusion. The first thing to do was to get out of the wood. At the people's urging, I had just parted company with my old boss and comrade, Harry Nkumbula because I had reluctantly decided that he was tired, drained of ideas and without any clear sense of direction. It hardly seemed wise to leave the people to get through the wilderness following one blind guide, Nkumbula, – the other, me, having perversely plucked out his eyes in obedience to some inner voice. That at least is how I saw things. Obviously, Mr Narayan must follow his star and I mine.

That meeting with Mr Narayan taught me a lesson or two about non-violence which took a long time to permeate my system. And in the years since, life, like a cane-wagging schoolmaster, has dinned into me the salient points whenever I was in danger of forgetting them. From time to time, other Narayans have crossed my path and invited me to abandon my chosen trade as a journeyman-politician for a better one. I do not know why it is that I seem to be thrown into contact constantly with *gurus*,

21

priests and philosophers with a passionate desire to save me from my worst self and recruit me for the cause. I am frequently told, for the good of my soul, that I am too kind, too other-worldly, too idealistic, too impractical, too religious to be a political leader. I suspect that deep down, they think I am too inept at *my* trade but might make out at *theirs*. I like the company of these mystics, seers and assorted saints and enjoy arguing with them but I have no immediate plans to take holy orders.

The Either-Or of Non-violence

However, to revert to Mr Narayan. He was inviting me, as others have done since, to make an either-or choice between an uncompromising stand on the issue of non-violence and pushing ahead with a political career which must lead me occasionally to do things at odds with my convictions. I could never see the issue in such stark either-or terms. Take, for instance, the case of the very movement Mr Narayan was representing, the Reverend Michael Scott's International Peace Brigade. In the event, the Brigade never marched. That is no disgrace. At least its members cared enough about our plight to do something about it. The reasons why the Peace Brigade disbanded are history now and need not concern us. But supposing it *had* marched, infiltrated Northern Rhodesia and fetched up in the streets of Lusaka, and suppose the Governor or Sir Roy Welensky* had obligingly lowered the flag and handed over the instruments of power. What then? The politicians having

---

* Sir Roy Welensky was Prime Minister of the Federation of Rhodesia and Nyasaland 1956-63, of which Northern Rhodesia, later Zambia, was a part.

been urged to abandon their trade and join the ranks of the moralists, who would have done all the sordid things needed to build good government and ensure the survival of the nation?

This is the problem of all protest movements which set their targets very high and claim to succeed where the politicians have failed. They hope to bridge the gap between warring factions by the appeal to a common interest that lies beyond conflict. And so long as they are stating broad though obvious truths at a time when people are sick of violence, they will have success as they are able to fire the public imagination and meet the mood of the moment. But when the marching stops, where do they go from there? Once the general mood has to become earthed, as it were, in practical action, then the movement's unity becomes shaky and political party loyalties revive. Party divisions are not always or even usually manufactured by politicians, though these wily birds may exploit them; parties generally reflect deep conflicts of human interest which can only be dealt with head-on. They will not go away like a marauding leopard scared off by the beating of drums and the waving of flags.

I have sworn never to fish in the troubled waters of someone else's country, having myself often been on the receiving end of unasked-for advice. But the Peace Movement of Northern Ireland seems to illustrate my point well. As a humanitarian, I have a great concern for its success, and as a practical politician I have stood where its members now stand – in No Man's Land between hostile armies. Racism or sectarianism – the stakes are the same, the survival of the nation as a human rather than sub-human enterprise. The courage, hope and love of the Peace People are beyond praise. But as they know better than I, they have reached the point where the marching has to stop and the perplexing question faced: what do we do now? No matter how disillusioned they may be with governments and politicians, they will find that politics is the only effective way of getting certain things done. Earnest dialogue alone will not heal deep divisions centuries old. The options are stark. The movement can keep its unity of purpose by turning its attention to uncontroversial projects in the field of education, community affairs and so on, and leave politics to the politicians – hardly a congenial idea since it was out of a conviction the old politics are dead that the movement came into being. Or else the movement will change into being a political party with a good chance that all the deep wounds of sectarian divisions will open up again.

I have no wish to sell short movements such as the Peace People. At the very least they help to create a climate in which people allow themselves to think about the hitherto unattainable. I simply want to make the point that politics will out, and therefore the either-or thinking of Mr Narayan, if taken seriously, would rob political life of its idealists without affecting the need for politicians as such. If the good man in politics quits the field, he leaves the more cynical of the breed to do as they like.

As I reflect now upon my experiences during Zambia's freedom struggle, I realize that non-violence is an exercise in public relations. It is often much else as well – a philosophy of life, a willingness to make heroic sacrifice, a religious vocation – but as a tactic its success or failure hangs on whether the offending regime can be shamed or spurred by outraged public opinion into putting its house in order. Thus a free press and all the gadgetry of the television age are as vital to the protest as the protesters themselves.

In one way, the Mahatma Gandhi and I were equally fortunate in facing a colonial power which fell far short of being a ruthless tyranny. Britain has always been very sensitive to public opinion – that is one of her glories. So the Viceroy who allowed reporters and even film cameramen into Gandhi's cell was inadvertently contributing to the effectiveness of the Mahatma's campaign of passive resistance. I too knew that all that happened to myself and my comrades during our non-violent struggle was shown within hours on British TV and reported over the radio and in the newspapers. I was able in this way to state my case not only throughout Zambia but also in London at the heart of empire. Had our struggle been in the Republic of South Africa or Salazaar's Portuguese African colonies, it might have been a different story. For every Steve Biko whose terrible fate gets world headlines, hundreds of his comrades vanish off the face of the earth, disciples of Gandhi and believers in armed struggle alike. By the eyes of God their courage and sacrifice are seen and noted, but politically, what the world does not know, it does not get worked up about.

Saints and Sinners in Politics

The politician's habit of weighing the odds before acting infuriates the saint – I use the word 'saint' loosely to mean someone who bases his entire life upon the unwavering acceptance of a moral principle such as that of non-violence;

one whose personal values, religious convictions and political actions are all of a piece, organized around that one theme. The saint is the man or woman who is too good for politics. I do not mean to be ironic. The saint finds the rules of the political game totally frustrating; the politician's caution and pragmatism he denounces as cynicism and time-serving. According to the saint, the politician will do the right thing so long as the way is easy and likely to bring him popularity, but when things get rough or complicated, he finds good reasons for choosing the broad path of compromise, and so betrays his principles.

There is some truth in that charge. How could it be otherwise? The politician is a human being – but he has a better excuse than that! He has trained himself to think of achievement in terms of getting things done. For him, the key question is not: is my motive pure and my heart at peace with the universe? but: what will happen if I do that rather than this? I think this is a proper question because it is rare that a political decision or action can be demonstrated from first principles to be right or wrong. Only in the light of the consequences of carrying it into effect can its value be seen. This is why so much squabbling about ideology is a waste of time. A particular monetary policy, for instance, whatever its advocates may say, is not graven in the heavens as part of holy writ. Either the policy works or it does not; either the nation and its people benefit from it or they do not. That seems to the politician to be the acid test. But such a yardstick is abhorrent to the saint who sees things quite differently. So be it – he has his destiny.

This disagreement between the politician and the saint reaches its climax where the great issues of life and death hang in the balance. Take for instance the significance of Gandhi's campaign of passive resistance in the 1930s. The politician studies the context and consequences of that slice of history before deciding whether it can become a model for action. The saint pooh-poohs all talk of historical comparison. He is interested primarily in the disposition of heart of the various contenders in a battle of wills. Ought one to give the greater weight to the Mahatma's motives or the results of his actions? The politician is bound to conclude that Gandhi's fate would have been quite different if instead of being up against the British Raj he had faced dictators who do not play good-natured games with their opponents. To the saint, such considerations are irrelevant. Gandhi living and dying by *satyagraha* is the thing which counts. His actions had a moral beauty and power which mock questions of short term material benefit. Just so, but there are other scales than the eternal by which the worth of our actions must be measured.

This is a very painful thing for me. Because I became known as an advocate of non-violence during Zambia's freedom struggle, my stand on the Rhodesia question has shocked and hurt some erstwhile allies who feel that I have let down myself and the whole cause of non-violence by my support for armed struggle. I do not think that anything I can say will reassure them, but I should like to try.

It is right that the tactics of a saint should remain the same whatever the nature of the challenge he faces. He believes flexibility of response is nothing more than evidence of easily manipulated conscience. For him, there is an absolute moral distinction between the methods of violence and non-violence, so to trim his position according to circumstances is not just pragmatism; it betrays the very

27

principle of his life. I cannot make this absolute moral distinction and feel it would be madness not to decide what response is likely to be effective in the light of the nature of the problem. Passive resisters, I am sure, did their part in the freedom struggle in Zimbabwe, but the sad truth is that Mr Smith was not shamed into giving house room in his mind to what a few years ago would have been unthinkable – the end of white domination. He was driven there by the freedom fighters who made his position untenable. For years, the rebel Rhodesian leader was deaf to the pleas, protests and righteous indignation of the world community. It was the sound of gunfire right outside his front door that convinced him the party was over – his attempt to detach Rhodesia from the rest of Africa had failed.

I shall have much more to say about the freedom struggle in Southern Africa and my attitude to it. For the time being, I merely observe that any *tactic* whether passive resistance or some other (and if any should deny the term 'tactic' and insist on 'gospel' or 'absolute law' then we must part company with mutual regret) becomes self-defeating if used at the wrong time and in the wrong way. Passive resistance may strengthen an oppressive authority if it diverts the people's righteous anger into easily controlled channels. On the other hand, badly directed armed struggle, besides costing many lives, may set back the cause a long way by giving government the excuse to rid itself of its most dangerous opponents. According to *Ecclesiastes*, to everything there is a season, and so with resistance. I believe there is a time to use the methods of passive resistance and a time to use those of armed struggle. And our discussion can only move forward if my critics will allow that this is at least a tenable position which should be subjected to keen analysis rather than head shaking disapproval.

I repeat: as a responsible politician I must always ask the question: will this or that *work*? Not is it noble in conception, sound in theory, highly desirable in the eyes of God – though I would dare hope for that too – but has it the remotest chance of changing things fundamentally? If it has not or if the degree of risk is unacceptable, then I have no right to sanction it. Not as a political leader. As a moralist, preacher, evangelist, I may plead any cause, however hazardous. But the people have asked the politician to help them achieve certain specific down-to-earth goals. They are not asking for a life of high moral risk, still less one of great sacrifice. Why should they? If the state is in great danger a leader may have to ask them for heroic deeds, but he must never forget that they are citizens and not martyrs. Some may become martyrs, and that must be a matter of personal choice – they cannot be ordered to go to the stake – except in that terrible eventuality where the state's very existence is under threat. Bare survival comes first. Of course, one would wish for more – that we might create a *just* state. But first it must survive.

Let me not overstate the degree of antithesis between the strategies of non-violence and those of armed struggle. It does not always follow that the way of non-violence is the more perilous. There may be times when it is the only sane course of action. Nor is armed struggle always the guarantor of national security. Far from it. But any leader must have the freedom to *discriminate*. I know that word sounds like a fall from grace into the grey areas of political morality. Alas, much of my life is spent in these murky waters.

29

More about the difference between the saint's followers and the politician's. Every brave spirit in the saint's army, who follows him to glory in the mouth of the guns, is a volunteer, spiritually equipped for the struggle and a fervent believer in the higher purpose he is serving. My constituency is a conscript army. I did not choose all of them – they happened to be born within the national boundaries of Zambia. They did not sign on for a death or glory struggle; in fact, they put me in my job because they thought it would lessen their chances of having to live dangerously – which does not make them cowards but prudent, sensible citizens.

My followers are a cross-section of humanity, saints and rogues, idealists and realists, believers and non-believers. They ask for a quiet life, reasonable prosperity and a secure future. As it is, I had to push their goodwill to the limit on the Zimbabwe issue. My fellow countrymen have borne the brunt of economic sanctions, the closing of the border, the pressure of a flood-tide of refugees on scarce resources. Later, they were even dying in their own land under a hail of rebel Rhodesia Air Force bombs. They have put up with a great deal out of solidarity with their brothers and sisters throughout Southern Africa, so it would be a monstrous thing to give the impression that the masses cannot rise above the basest levels of human existence. But they have the right to eat the fruit of their suffering, not in some other world from which strife and trouble are excluded, but in the here and now. I do not have a low view of the people; quite the contrary, which is why I must take with the utmost seriousness their deepest wishes and hopes.

Gandhi's *satyagraha* campaigns in the 1930s seem to refute the point I am making. Apparently he was able to inspire a whole people to accept the way of sacrifice. I think that Gandhi was unique, and at least in this case his methods were not for export. He was the holiest of men in a country which venerated holy men and gave them extraordinary respect and authority. There was the psychic strength of India's ancient religion which filled the souls of even the poorest of people with powerful impulses towards purity and truth. There was the British Raj, going through that period the biblical Samson must have known well, conscious of its fading strength. And then there was Nehru and the Indian National Congress banging away in the wings, behaving like an orthodox freedom movement, able to consolidate the gains made through *satyagraha* and acting as a warning to the ruling power what was likely to happen if Gandhi's methods did not succeed. These things came together in one place and time. All this may be special pleading but I do not think so.

As a political leader I have no right to lead my conscript army into battles we have little chance of winning because of some conviction that defeat will be a great tonic for their spirits. I know the saint finds talk of 'acceptable risk' and 'possible consequences' exasperating. His battle cry is: 'If it is right, do it and hang the consequences!' I have read that people in the town of Kitty Hawk used to taunt the Wright Brothers as they tried to make an aeroplane with the cry, 'That thing will never fly!' The aviation pioneers had enough faith in their contraption to believe they were taking an acceptable risk in leaving the ground. But had they responded to their critics by saying, 'We have no idea whether this thing will fly or not, nor have we any real interest in that question. It's the principle that counts, so roll up and bring along your families for a joy ride!' that

31

would be a gamble of a different order. I need not labour the point.

The Machine Age Heresy

There is a dangerous tendency in some circles to apply the laws of the Machine Age to the business of government. I suppose the basic tenet of applied science is that there is no such thing as an insoluble problem. Unless something is inherently absurd, sooner or later someone is going to find a way of doing it. All that is needed is more brain power, more money, more equipment, more hard work. This is a fine, brave philosophy when applied to the world of things. It can be very dangerous when introduced into the world of politics. I would term it the Machine Age heresy, and it is dangerous because it can raise false hopes, foster illusions, and above all, lead to the drawing of conclusions prematurely before all the evidence is in – 'since there has got to be a solution, *this* must surely be it!'

I have learned that in the world of politics, whatever may be the case in the world of science, there are certain problems which at any given time are strictly insoluble. It is not a question of thinking and working harder, of using more brain power or applying greater resources. There is something missing – a Factor X – without which no solution is possible. Factor X may simply be time – time for the healing of old wounds and the obliteration of hateful memories, time for a generation to arise which does not cherish old animosities. Factor X may be many things, but for lack of it, some great besetting problem in the world of human affairs remains intractible. We must simply live

32

with it as best we can, using our best efforts to tease out a solution but remaining modest in expectation and yet hopeful in spite of our bafflement. I would submit that there are a number of great issues of foreign affairs that fall into the category of the strictly insoluble at the present time – and any attempt to apply the Machine Age heresy and foreclose our options could well be disastrous. This is not to suggest that we do nothing and freeze for a couple of generations into yoga-like stillness. Balance is everything.

As I see it, when the saint in politics comes up against an unsolved problem, he produces his Factor X as a universal nostrum. It may be non-violence or class struggle or negritude or whatever. But he is so passionately committed to this master idea that he cannot imagine circumstances where it would be inappropriate. When I was a child, the *nganga* in the village had one remedy for all ills, goat dung. Whether you went along complaining about your eyes, or stomach, or feet, it made no difference. The answer was always goat dung. Possibly sometime in the past he had achieved an amazing cure using goat dung and so it became for him the key to the riddle of the universe.

This insistence upon applying Factor X to any problem makes the saint an inflexible though high-principled politician. He has a bright, terrible vision. So intently does he gaze into the sun that he trips over tree roots. His zeal is only a few degrees in intensity short of fanaticism and his use of power becomes ever more authoritarian. He becomes a dictator for God's sake or humanity's. He is travelling as straight as an arrow, but in a bent world. We craftier politicians, having discovered that the world *is* bent, or as the preacher would put it, fallen, take the precaution of putting some spin on the ball before we send it speeding to its target. But an inflexible truth, pursued single-mindedly through a complex world, is always in danger of changing, unnoticed, into a terrible error. The true way lies between saintly illusion and political cynicism – the illusion, that we can mould the world according to our vision; the cynicism, that of scaling down our visions to the level of what the world will accept as practicable.

History, I think, supports the view that the saint in power tends to create an authoritarian regime. So drunk is he with the truth he sees, that if he cannot get the people to see it too he will put out their eyes to aid their vision. If they will not freely reply, 'Amen', to the creed he recites, then they must be encouraged with hot irons – for the good of their souls, of course. In fact, the more I see the saint, eaten up with zeal, heading off to glory in spite of the odds, the more I come to value cowardice or at least the capacity to perform a graceful *volte face* as a political virtue. I recall those dangerous days when President Kennedy gave Mr Kruschev an ultimatum to dismantle Soviet missile sites in Cuba or else. The world trembled on the lip of war. Then Kruschev capitulated and the sites were dismantled and shipped back to Russia. President Kennedy was widely praised for his firmness. But to my mind, Mr Kruschev deserved at least two cheers for his willingness to undergo the odium of apparent defeat rather than stick doggedly to a path that could only lead to world war.

Nearer to home. . . . when rebel Rhodesian Air Force jets first bombed refugee camps in Zambia in October 1978, I refused to order any retaliatory strike. International pacifist organizations congratulated me on my forbearance. Alas, I did not deserve their applause. Zambia had not the weaponry to sustain all-out war, and that is what would have been involved. Only a fool goes willingly into a war he cannot win. On the other hand, there is a propaganda war to be won and it is important not to lose the moral advantage of being the injured party, especially when world opinion is such an important factor in the equation. I was reacting as a politician rather than a saint, though I would like to think that at the end of the day the welfare of my fellow countrymen was best served by discretion even if their pride was bruised. Before going in for sabre-rattling, it is wise to make sure your side has the biggest sabres.

From Movement to Government

Do I sing a different song now from the days when my political party, the United National Independence Party, was acting on an official policy of non-violence and used it to achieve a virtually bloodless victory in the independence struggle? I believe not. A freedom movement has not the same mandate for power as a government; no political party's interests can be exactly identical with those of the state; the ultimate sanctions are not as severe, and the price of a mistake is not so calamitous.

All this I have learned through a course of very tough lessons in the years since Zambia became independent in 1964.

As leader of a political movement I could choose the tools with which to set about the job in hand, according to my estimate of the difficulty of the task, my own temperamental inclinations and moral scruples. Every one of those who followed me did so of his or her free will. There were no passengers, no reluctant recruits, no conscripts. And of course our goal was limited – a great, awe-inspiring goal, but limited – to free Zambia from colonial rule and establish an independent republic. All our energy was brought to a burning focus on that one point. True, we had our party conferences at which we argued for a long time about education, health, economics and so on. Some of our brightest ideas have vanished without trace, others have had to be put to the hard test of practicability in Government policies. But it is true to say that our absorbing interest was always on the issue of independence and how it was to be achieved. We never strayed far from that tantalizing question.

Once we took over government, we moved into a strange, new world where all the rules of the game were different. I suppose soldiers in battle look back upon their peace-time manoeuvres as though they were a dream – 'casualties' get to their feet when the exercise is over, guns make loud bangs but hurt no one. Then comes the time of the men who fall never to rise again, of real blood, of the sorrow of loss or the excitement of having survived. That is how we felt as we walked for the first time through the government buildings that had for so long housed the teachers who became our enemies – a sense that it was not really true; we would be back at the compound on the black side of town when someone blew a whistle and pronounced the game over.

My friend Fenner Brockway recalls the day when the early Socialists first got their hands on a parliamentary seat and finally on the Government itself, and the extraordinary feelings – excitement and anti-climax – when what had seemed an impossible prize was theirs. We had even more cause for amazement: we had not only dislodged a great imperial power but had given the lie to centuries of propaganda which told us we would always be the underdogs.

They were wonderful moments, but followed by a sense of fear – like sitting on the flight deck of a Concorde in the air and knowing that every button you touch is 'live'. It is not some game or test, things will happen which have to be right because they cannot be made to unhappen. I was untried in the arts of statecraft. I was not the son of a chief of the old Africa trained from childhood by the elders for the task of ruling. Nor was I a Winston Churchill, who seemed for much of his adult life to have been either in the corridors of power or just outside them, in and out of numerous governments and when not actually Prime Minister rubbing shoulders with those who were. Abraham Lincoln went from Log Cabin to White House; I moved backwards, if the names are anything to go by, from 'Galilee' (the name of our little home) to State House – Lubwa Mission to the Presidential Office. It was a frightening leap.

The business of statecraft is enough to sober the keenest idealist. For all the brave and sincere talk about the democratic process and the importance of free consent, the great levers of power operate not far below the surface of things, and the first illusion the leader must banish is his fond hope that he need not touch them; that he can get things done simply by persuasion. Not every citizen is a convert to the new regime; some will do their duty with the greatest reluctance; many will find measures that strike at their pockets or freedoms hard to bear; all will have something to grumble about.

For the first time, the leader feels isolated from the people. He is cut off not only by the trappings of office but

by the sense that whereas once he did things gladly together
with them for choice, now things must be done by regula-
tion for reasons that may not be obvious or understood.
Once I had incited the people to refuse to pay taxes to the
Federation of Rhodesia and Nyasaland whose existence we
refused to acknowledge; now I must insist that my fellow
tax-dodgers pay up to support the State of Zambia. Once
we boycotted schools as a protest against discrimination
in education, but what was then an act of free defiance
now became an offence – 'Children must go to school!'
Kaunda's law says! It is the sheer power of the state, and
the inevitability of that power which awes the new leader.
And yet, should he ever lose that sense of awe and become
matter of fact about power, or even develop an appetite for
pulling those levers, then he is a menace – there is a mad
man, in political terms, at the helm.

Not only is power everywhere around the leader of a new
state, but the ditches along which much of it flows have
been dug by his predecessors. No state, however revolutionary its founding doctrine, emerges brand-new from the
package. Mao Tse-tung brought the world's biggest
nation into the twentieth century and rid it of the whole
gang of colonialists, war lords and capitalist pirates. But the
new China is still the old China, the China of the dynastic
emperors and philosophers, of long traditions and ancient
religions. The depth and thickness of the roots under the
ground determine the direction in which the tree will
spread, just as any blight on those roots must eventually
discolour its leaves. I certainly found this too. Zambia
had a new name, constitution, government and ruling
philosophy, but we inherited obligations which went
further back than the colonialists or even the earliest

African tribesmen. They had to do with our history, geography, climate, the quality of our soil, the wealth or poverty of natural resources.

These obligations issued in international treaties, trade links, economic policies and so on. We could not reverse the flow of the Zambezi by an act of our Assembly when we became independent, so we were dependent for much hydro-electric power on the Rhodesians. We could not sell our copper at street corners in Lusaka and so had to continue our membership of a very complex international commodity market. We could not compensate in a year or two for the decades of educational neglect that had left our people disadvantaged, especially in technical and scientific skills, and so we still had to rely on some expatriate technologists – and pay them well for their work. So another source of social and political stress remained beyond independence – preferential treatment, except before the law, for whites. But what were we to do? The economic and technical infra-structure of our country was created before we took over. We inherited it, and had to ensure it did not collapse for we had neither time nor resources to build another. And so it goes.

These hard facts of life must be faced by the leader whose people are sure to feel he is bending over too much in the direction of the past instead of wiping the slate clean and beginning again. Would that one could! But these accommodations with harsh reality must be made, no matter how much the saint alleges in disgust that one has broken with strict principle. The only *strict* principles are in text books.

History as well as experience shows that the younger the nation, the nearer the surface are the roots of violence. We look upon the United States these days as the oldest democracy and as a mature and humane nation, Vietnam notwithstanding. But if one reads Tocqueville's observations on the country when he encountered it in the nineteenth century, it is hard to recognize in the picture he draws the 'Sweet Land of Liberty'. Commenting on the extermination of the American Indians, he writes, 'The Americans accomplished this thing in the cleverest way imaginable – calmly, legally, philanthropically, without bloodshed and, so far as the world could see, without violating a single great moral principle. It would be impossible to think of a better way of destroying people and at the same time exhibiting higher respect for the laws of humanity'. What makes the story of the obliteration of the Indians so terrible is that it was all done for the best of motives, using the full majesty of the law and in the name of Christianity.

The moral to someone like myself is obvious. We must be constantly alert not simply for that naked and crude misuse of power that results from our selfishness and arrogance, but also for the more subtle violence which is the consequence of our idealism and determination to do others good even if we must kill them in the attempt. And this danger is at its most acute in our earliest days when we have the sun upon our faces and our hopes are high and we have not yet learned the hard way just what are the limits of effective government.

Living by the Sword

A German thinker has written, 'He who affirms the state, affirms violence'. And which of us does not affirm the state? Maybe with fear and loathing, with tears in our eyes, but we affirm it all right. There are small communities of very religious people, saints in fact, who have from time to time taken themselves off to remote places, away from the tyranny of persecution perhaps, or else to try to work out on the ground some blueprint derived from the Bible or some other sacred writing. They swear never to draw the sword again, to foreswear all the apparatus of the police and law and compulsion, to live in primitive, free goodwill, all serving the cause of each; each willingly sacrificing his own interests for those of the whole community. Unfortunately, such Shangri-Las never last. They usually collapse because weak human beings cannot bear indefinitely the burden of superhuman expectations their leaders lay upon them.

So far as I know, no state has managed to survive for long without the use of compulsion, including if necessary, violence. Some people draw a comforting distinction between 'force' and 'violence'. They define 'violence' as the improper use of 'force', and 'force' as 'violence sanctioned by the law'. I refuse to cloud the issue by such word-play. Anything which hurts a human being is violence, and there is no point in beating about the bush. With some exceptions, the power which establishes a state is violence; the power which maintains it is violence; the power which eventually overthrows it is violence – or if you prefer a nicer word 'force'. Of course, we must make judgements about types of violence and the degree of guilt that should attach to each, but I do not see how we can face squarely our political responsibilities unless we see sombre realities as they are without blurring the definitions. Call an elephant a rabbit only if it gives you comfort to feel that you are about to be trampled to death by a rabbit.

41

The law of inherited obligations applies particularly to the use of force. When we took over Zambia, we climbed on to an escalator already on the move, by which I mean that Zambia like every other state was already caught up in the vicious circle of violence – that endless chain of retaliation which stretches back to Cain. And we could not, any more than our predecessors, break the chain, saying in effect, 'Well, we had to use a reasonable amount of violence to fight our way into the Promised Land, but now we've arrived we can beat our swords into ploughshares and sit under our fig trees in peace'. In the very act of battling towards our goal we have given the deadly wheel of violence another turn. One may hope to liberalize the state by good government, to encourage a deeper culture, a broader civilization, but over everything hangs the shadow of the sword. I read in *Revelations* that in the New Jerusalem there is neither temple nor sword, which I take to mean that both the State and the Church have been declared redundant and replaced by a free fellowship of loving spirits.

I look forward to that happy time and trust I shall be found worthy of walking the streets of the New Jerusalem and sharing in the life of the fellowship of free spirits. But I do not really think we can leave matters there. It would be irresponsible not to take seriously these pessimistic judgements about the state and the universal persistence of violence. But we must not be totally conditioned by them, otherwise what would there be left worth fighting for on earth? The Bible tells us we shall only see the Kingdom of Heaven in all its fullness and perfection in heaven but we must not make that an excuse for sitting back, allowing our animal nature full rein and relying on God alone to clean up the whole earthly creation and make it fit to be his dwelling hereafter. Otherwise I do not see the point of all Jesus's preaching of the gospel of the Kingdom of Heaven. He talked of very little else. He told us to seek first the Kingdom of Heaven and to pray for its coming so that God's will might be done on earth as it is in heaven. We must not cut the nerve between our heavenly hopes and our earthly struggle to make the world a better place and advance man's spiritual and material development.

Of course Jesus's choice of the image of the Kingdom of Heaven does not mean that he thought of God's will being done on earth exclusively through some sort of political arrangement – turning the Gospel, in fact, into a political manifesto. We must not make the mistake of identifying the Kingdom of Heaven with any ideology or political philosophy. That way lies fascism. Nevertheless, I do not think Jesus was solely concerned with individual morality and holiness. The ultimate state of blessedness on earth is to be able to love God with all our heart and mind and soul and strength and our neighbour as ourselves. Now if such a wonderful state has no effect upon our organized political, social and economic life then I and all those who share my search for the Kingdom of Heaven are wasting our time.

I do not believe I am wasting my time. I have great faith in my fellow men and women and believe there can be no higher vocation than that of trying to create the conditions of life which enable them to be fully human. This is not just a political goal, it has profound religious significance. Everything we do which makes it easier for men and women to show love towards one another enables them, however imperfectly, to share the life of God who is Love. When man learns, by bitter experience if in no other way, that the only hope for the peace and happiness of the world is to give social and political and economic expression to love for others, we shall be in the presence not of the Kingdom of Man but the Kingdom of God.

I believe that man is still evolving, not physically but spiritually – the changes now take place in his mind and soul rather than in his biological make-up. This higher form of evolution unlike the earlier stages, is a matter of individual choice rather than inevitable, unseen rather than obvious and brought about not by the raw force of nature but by the agency of love. It might be called the survival of the highest rather than the survival of the fittest. Of course it would be foolish to claim that we are wiser or better in a moral sense than our ancestors, yet I do believe we understand more about ourselves and our place in the universe. And we can trace the evolution of our conscience even through the legal structures of our society. We no longer regard slavery, the subordination of women, child labour and racial discrimination as either inevitable or desirable. I work and pray for the time when the evolution of our conscience will take us to the point where we see war as a wasteful and degrading thing and dare to hope we can outgrow the need for violence.

So I am torn between the need to make somewhat gloomy though I think realistic assessments of the nature of the state and a kind of soaring optimism about man which comes from my Christian faith. I do not think this tension can ever be fully resolved and we must live with it as best we can. The statesman and humble believer are at odds not simply in the same state but within the one person. At all costs the two halves of the paradox of man's heavenly hopes and earthly striving must be held together. Without political realism the people are in mortal peril; without an equally firm commitment to worldly idealism there is no goal worth struggling for. Hence, whenever I am required to wrestle in my mind and heart with dark realities such as the present inevitability of violence, as an antidote I always preach myself a little sermon on the glory and possibilities of man made in God's image.

The Perfect Law and Imperfect Men

What room is there then for the saint in politics? The cynic would say that politics provides a job for fallen saints—politicians retire into sainthood when they are too old to do any further damage. I believe the saint by his loyalty to an inflexible principle, his refusal to compromise, his unwillingness to bend the knee before the hard truths I have been trying to state, is witnessing to a perfect law in an imperfect world. And the Old Testament has some fascinating examples of the relationship between the leader and the saint, or, in its terms, between king and prophet. The king tries to rule as best he can, playing his political games, cutting his corners, coming to terms with the devil from time to time, whilst the prophet calls down the wrath of God upon the king for his miserable performance and infringement of God's law. And the king shows that he is still obedient, not entirely beyond hope, by allowing the prophet to speak uncomfortable words and listening carefully to him. So highly do I rate this role that if I were asked to point to the mark of a 'Christian' society in terms of leadership, I would say it is one that has, not necessarily a Christian ruler in the palace but a Christian prophet within earshot of him.

But the saint or prophet (I seem to have promoted him – the two are one – the prophet is a saint wearing a political hat) will be effective only if he foreswears any political ambition, holds to his course in spite of everything and, above all, refuses to sell his principles in the market-place alongside the rest of us.

Of course the saint will remind us that if only men and women would love one another there would be no need for violence. Of course the politician will retort that the saint's 'if' begs the most important question in a fallen world. For it is precisely because men and women are sinful that they cannot live by the law of love in community. Yet the saint is doing his job in keeping before us the perfect law of God. He is saying in effect that the world is sinful, but it is not only sinful, it is also being redeemed; men and women who choose the way of love do not have to protect themselves or expect the state to protect them, there is another option – martyrdom. And *the* most important thing the Christian saint is saying by his refusal to compromise is that it is not by political, military or economic means that we can break out of the vicious circle of violence but by follow-ing the way of the Cross. 'The Old Rugged Cross' was the first hymn I learned to play on my guitar at Lubwa. I did not imagine then that its simple words would go round and round in my head and haunt my dreams years later.

I have two nagging problems I am always anxious to debate with the saint. In inviting us to follow the way of the Cross, is he not asking people who are not Christian to behave as though they were? Why should they? I think that the first act of non-violence some saints need to per-form is to stop asking others to behave as though they were saints too. My second problem stems from the first. If it is true that the only effective alternative to violence is to accept the way of the Cross, how do we get the nation as opposed to individuals to follow it? By definition it is a government's task to see to it that the state survives, not to encourage it to perish by its own hand. This prompts the thought of the ultimate absurdity – can it ever be right for a leader to *compel* his people to follow the way of the Cross? The Cross surely, is a saving act because it is freely chosen, otherwise it is just a horrible form of execution.

The saint, I think, wishes to make a political platform out of personal martyrdom. I think he is wrong. But the possibility must be considered, not as an exercise in theory, but against the background of Southern Africa as a whole and my people in particular, caught in the violence trap, and bleeding.

PART TWO

The Disciple's Dilemma

During 1958 the independence struggle threatened to get out of hand. There was trouble between the police and some of our followers in the Northern Province and the mood in the towns was one of sullen anger. Welensky's army dashed about the place like columns of enraged ants and armed guards were placed on public buildings. I was afraid that long suppressed indignation would explode into civil war. The British Government must also have been alarmed because they asked the Governor of Northern Rhodesia, Sir Arthur Benson, to meet Harry Nkumbula and myself and hear our views on constitutional change.

For the first time in the Territory's history, two black men went to Government House to put an ultimatum rather than beg favours or pay respects. Nkumbula and I were very nervous, but we were determined not to be overawed as we passed through the huge portico – two rows of high pillars obviously built to intimidate any troublesome natives trying to lay hands on the Queen's representative. Now my grandchildren and their friends play hide and seek there and I fancy the ghosts of those proud colonial governors cry out in pain . . . on second thoughts, probably not! They had such iron-clad social confidence that nothing could embarrass them.

Sir Arthur was, as always, courteous and rather remote.

In those days the British Raj did not say much. If you were good, it smiled approvingly; if not, its frown made you feel that three hundred years of imperial history had dropped out of the skies on to your head. Just like the boarding master at Munali, my old school, praising the prefects for keeping order in the dormitory after Lights Out, Sir Arthur announced that he was pleased with us – we seemed to be behaving in such a moderate and responsible manner. His smile vanished when we told him of our people's demands – an end to Federation, an early date for independence and an election based on One Man One Vote. He heard us out and then said to me. 'Mr Kaunda, don't you realize the whites would paralyse government if we accepted your demands?'. I replied, 'Are you saying, Your Excellency, that for our demands to be met, *we* have got to be in a position to paralyse government?'. He did not answer.

But there, in a short snatch of conversation, is set out the dilemma of the disciple of non-violence. The tyrant (in this case a fairly mild one) pats him on the head for being a good chap and keeping off the rough stuff, but all the time he is lavishing praise on the man of peace he is really paying attention to the man of war whose slightest move galvanizes him into action.

The ambiguous attitude of the rulers of this world towards non-violence was well illustrated following the murder of Dr Martin Luther King. President Lyndon B. Johnson praised the dead leader to the skies for his steadfast witness to non-violence, extolling the moral and spiritual value of the lives of those who would prefer to suffer violence than offer it. But at the very time he was affirming the power and truth of non-violence, President Johnson was busy stepping up the American war effort in South-

East Asia. Underneath the fine talk, the President was really saying that whilst he saluted Martin Luther King for offering only peaceful opposition to the US Government, the Johnson Administration had no intention of doing unto the Viet Cong and North Vietnamese as it had been done unto by Dr King. In other words, non-violence is what any civilized opponent *ought* to use against us; regretfully, we have no alternative but to use violence against our opponent because he is just not civilized – obviously not, otherwise he would not be opposing us.

It is not pleasant for the disciple of non-violence to be patronized by supercilious opponents nor does he enjoy being written off as a fool and a weakling by some of his comrades, but these things he can put up with. What he finds truly agonizing is the realization that try as he will to distance himself from all violence in thought and deed, he cannot. For violence and non-violence, far from being absolute alternatives, are complementary in practice. As a tactic, the effectiveness of non-violence is enhanced when it stands out in sharp relief against a backdrop of imminent or actual violence. It has been said that non-violence *needs* violence in the same way stars need the night sky to show them off.

My own experience bears out this truth. In the early days of the nationalist movement when I was trying to impress on our followers the importance of learning and practising the methods of non-violent struggle, my speeches were reported by the press in a semi-humorous way and I was lampooned as 'The Preacher'. I suppose I was regarded by those in power as a harmless crackpot. But then as things got bogged down and it looked as though Sir Roy Welensky and his Federal Government would succeed in holding

51

off our nation's independence indefinitely, sections of the Party's Youth Brigade lost patience. Instead of putting up quietly with all the provocation and racial taunts that were their daily lot, they retaliated and there were some very nasty incidents. Editorials in national newspapers argued that Kaunda was losing control of the Party and there was much gloom and doom talk about the prospect of civil war. And the same people who had earlier dismissed my advocacy of non-violence as silly sermonizing then turned round and reviled me for failing to get the Party to heed my preaching.

But official attitudes towards me changed radically. Whilst the Party was following instructions and avoiding violent confrontation I was shrugged aside as irrelevant; when widespread violence became a real possibility, I was suddenly seen as a rational alternative to the so-called 'men of violence'. By 'rational' of course the white settlers meant the black opponent least likely to cause them anxiety or threaten their privileged position. Martin Luther King noted a similar change in attitude on the part of the US Government following the black riots in Detroit and elsewhere. From being a localized nuisance he became something of a national hero because it is easier to cope with bus boycotts than the burning down of city ghettos. And I suspect that Gandhi and his *satyagraha* policy became much more attractive to the British Government when Nehru's National Congress began rioting in the streets. It is the stars and the dark night again – the play and counterplay of violence and non-violence. Just as the stars do not stop shining when the night has gone, so non-violence has its own validity quite apart from violence. Nonetheless, it is not wise for the pacifist to be too self-righteous about the 'men of violence' – their very existence often guarantees his effectiveness.

The other aspect of the dilemma of the political leader who chooses the way of non-violence concerns his relationship with his followers. The people want results, especially when they have been suffering oppression and the denial of their rights for years past. Indeed, had their impatience not reached boiling point the mass movement would probably not have come into existence at all. Western observers of Africa have a curious tendency to equate such impatience with immaturity. They claim that a more civilized people would possess their souls in patience whatever the provocation. Europe's recent history does not furnish very convincing evidence of this principle – was not Prime Minister Chamberlain reviled as the Great Appeaser for advocating just this sort of patience after Munich?

For years, right-wing politicians in Britain combined condemnation of black 'terrorist' action in Rhodesia with exhortations to the black population to bide their time until their betters decide they were ready for and deserving of basic human rights. I cannot imagine that great hero of British right-wing politicians, Sir Winston Churchill, telling the occupied peoples of Europe in 1940 to be patient and trust the Nazis to restore their freedom one day – maybe not in their own lifetime nor that of their children, but one day. Such patience would be neither noble nor civilized but the mark of a happy slave.

Once oppressed peoples wake up to the fact that it is not the law of God nor the nature of the universe that they should be treated as second-class human beings, then a single day of continued servitude becomes insupportable, let alone a lifetime of it. And even those too old to benefit much by self-determination themselves become impatient for it on behalf of their children and future generations yet unborn.

If to this impatience in the face of injustice is added the commonsense perception that the powerful never willingly give up power – it has to be taken from them, it is obvious that the mind of a people on the brink of a freedom struggle is not very hospitable to *any* long-term strategies, least of all those of non-violence, which mean delayed results and the suppression of honest feelings. So the leader of a mass movement, whatever path he chooses to follow, is living on borrowed time – he must get results before his followers' frustration explodes and he is swept aside. And if he is committed to a policy of non-violence, his political lifespan depends upon both his supporters *and* his opponents – his supporters, because there is a limit to the amount of knocking about without retaliation they are prepared to take from security forces who are not themselves committed to non-violence; and his opponents, in that they must be wise enough to make concessions willingly before they are compelled to do so. If, lulled into complacency by the apparent docility of the freedom movement, those in power refuse to make significant concessions, then the movement's leader will almost certainly fall and be replaced by someone pledged to get quick results at whatever cost in human life.

The problem with this line of argument is obvious – any ruling power which is wise enough to make sufficient concessions to vindicate non-violent opposition, would probably be wise enough in the first place to read the signs of the times and change things. There would be no need for any freedom movement outside the law, violent or non-violent. Otherwise, the gloomy law holds – normally, non-violent protest only gets results when it is seen by those in power as a desirable alternative to violence, and it only becomes desirable when the other alternative is being spelled out in blood.

A Sport for Gentlemen?

For what it is worth, I can claim to be one of the few national leaders who led a mass movement to victory in a freedom struggle, not only using the tactics of non-violence but actually having the principle written into my Party's constitution. And when in 1958 I quit the African National Congress and helped to form the United National Independence Party, I took that clause with me as part of my essential baggage. And at annual conferences, I and those of my colleagues who believed in the doctrine had to defend it against sceptics who argued that because the police and army did not practise non-violence our people were getting hurt; that the message from the rest of Africa and the whole colonial world was that freedom did not drop from a tree like an overripe avocado but had to be plucked. Furthermore, there was little evidence that non-violent, positive action was actually working. These were strong arguments, but we held the line and the clause has never been removed from our constitution, though once or twice it has been a close-run thing.

Much harder than winning debates at conferences was the business of schooling our ordinary members in the rules of non-violence. It was not too difficult getting the methods across but inculcating correct attitudes was a different matter. People instinctively react to provocation – do not the psychologists say that man's primitive response to danger is either fight or flight? And yet, paradoxically, though passivity is not natural in the face of violence it can become so as a result of centuries of repression. Passive resistance is not congenial to the rebellious poor because something of the sort has been the sorry story of their lives since time immemorial. When someone's jackboot is pressing your head into the dust, what option have you but to become pacifist? But once there is a surge of new consciousness which comes to a head in widespread rebelliousness then it is precisely this passivity which is being rejected. Supine acceptance of their historical fate is a demon which must be cast out of the people's souls before they will have the self-confidence to begin their crusade for freedom. To tell the masses who have screwed up their courage to the sticking point to be patient – though in a different way from their previous enforced patience – is a subtlety not easy to grasp.

Put another way – passive resistance is, amongst other things, a kind of communication, a system of gestures which must be received and understood. Now, if under a thousand beatings I have held my peace how does my oppressor know that I hold my peace on the thousandth and one occasion for a different reason? How is he to guess that my attitude this time is a planned response and not the dumb subservience of the past? Of course there is an important moral distinction between passive resistance and cowed passivity but if the difference is too subtle for a tyrant to grasp how will he get the message and change his ways?

I think the class aspect of this problem can be underestimated. Non violence relies for much of its effectiveness on shared attitudes and values between oppressors and those trying to change their minds. Take, for instance, South Africa. A white South African, protesting against his own government by being prepared to get hurt in demonstrations, go to gaol or even put his life at risk without retaliation, will make some impact on his fellow-whites, especially those who must deal with him, because they know precisely how he feels. They may not sympathize with the martyr's cause or even understand what possesses him to embrace it but they do understand that he *is* suffering and to this extent some moral pressure is being applied to them. When, however, a black South African submits willingly to being beaten up or humiliated in other ways, what's new? Since it is a hazard of daily living and likely to come his way whether he is a peaceful revolutionary or a casual passer-by who gets under a policeman's feet, who is to know that the victim is actually a martyr?

If you are a South African white entitled in the government's eyes to freedom, security and comfort, then any action you take which puts these things under threat will be recognized as costly if foolish. But if you are a black peasant taking the same action it will seem to be a distinction without a difference, but certainly not a sacrifice, should you freely exchange a sub-human existence in a rural kraal for a sub-human existence in gaol.

The most wretched soul on earth has, of course, one possession he can lay on the line as a gesture of sacrifice for his cause – his life. Martyrdom is always magnificent. I sometimes wonder whether *any* of the ideas that grip the mind of man is worth dying for, but I never doubt that it is worth dying for the right to hold that idea. And yet. . . . life is so cheap under many oppressive regimes that the would-be martyr has the duty of deciding whether his death is likely to be a sacrifice or a waste. There is a time to die just as there is a time to be born and he who anticipates it may be exercising a precious human right without doing much for the rights of others. So granted that it is a holy and a splendid thing for someone who has nothing else to give a cause to offer his life, I would suggest that a one-shot army which is wiped out in every battle is unlikely to have any of the future for whose sake the sacrifice is supposedly being made.

All this has led me to the conclusion that passive resistance is a sport for gentlemen (and ladies) – just like the pursuit of war, a heroic enterprise for the ruling classes but a grievous burden laid on the rest. To be effective (as opposed to worthwhile, which is not the same thing) passive resistance relies on the oppressor sticking to the same rules as those seeking to change him. Ironically, whilst much is said about the high moral quality of passive resistance, it is rarely acknowledged that it makes equally rigorous moral demands on the oppressor, who is expected to show a remarkable amount of magnanimity in not taking advantage of an opponent's helplessness. This prompts the question: if a tyrant is capable of such generosity, why is any form of conflict necessary at all other than a political struggle along conventional lines?

Wherever I have travelled throughout the world, pacifist groups have sought me out and I have been much impressed by their idealism and courage. I have been equally struck by similarities amongst the human types represented – usually professional, rarely peasant, generally religious and frequently politically innocent in the sense that they perceive simple solutions to complex problems – solutions which more often than not make superhuman demands upon ordinary people.

I fully realize that in making such harsh judgements about admirable people I am condemning myself, for I have been and would still claim to be one of them in spirit. But we must be free of illusion if we are to reclaim Southern Africa for sanity. And illusion, of a bourgeois kind, is a threat to be guarded against. For instance, take this strange notion that it is still possible to be free inside your head even though your conditions of life are intolerable – and that this inner freedom is the most important kind.

I have heard a lot about this 'internal' freedom of which no tyrant can rob us, and I think it is an illusion. Firstly, whilst it may be true that intensely creative people can live a life of the mind oblivious of all that goes on around them, this is a luxury denied to the masses. They live so near to starvation point that their ability to think about *anything* depends upon the arrival of the next meal. Anyone who has seen human wretches slumped in the torpor of semi-starvation would dismiss as nonsense talk about 'inner' freedom. When you know where your family's meal is coming from, have some kind of shelter from the elements and can see some release from grinding labour *then* you can start to explore your inner freedom.

The second reason why I think the concept of inner freedom is a bourgeois illusion is that it under-estimates the power of thought-control under despotism. Peoples subjected to British colonialism never experienced the horrors of mental torture through drugs, sleep deprivation and other methods associated with modern totalitarianism, yet we were the victims of thought-control through the educational system and discriminatory laws. We were in danger of having the desire for intellectual freedom bred out of us. Concepts such as 'superior' and 'inferior', 'freedom' and 'servitude', 'truth' and 'falsehood' were turned onto their heads and otherwise confused, so it was hard to know just what 'inner' freedom was.

My view therefore is that the distinction between 'inner' freedom and any other kind only has meaning for an intellectual or cultural elite. As for the rest of us – we must have freedom pure and simple, whole and undivided, or else we just are not free. So any philosophy of resistance which offers freedom in the depths of the heart alone – though that is important – is of little value to the masses.

A thoroughgoing pacifism also creates difficulties of a different kind for the practising politician – it encourages blanket judgements about political regimes, ruling out those marginal moral distinctions that are the raw stuff of statesmanship. Some pacifist literature boils down to saying that there is really nothing to choose between one side or the other in a conflict if force is used to resolve it. It is immaterial who wins, victory will be sterile because it was achieved by violence. This attitude makes the pacifist the dupe of totalitarianism because a strong despotic power very often does not need to use force to intimidate a weaker one whereas free nations mobilizing to resist such aggression have to marshal their military resources, and thus incur the pacifist's wrath. Hence, I read that when Hitler occupied the Rhineland in 1936 without firing a shot, the anger of European pacifists was aimed not at the Fuhrer for his territorial aggression, but at statesmen like Winston Churchill who argued that the Germans should be stopped by force before it was too late.

This uncritical condemnation of any regime which relies

on force would rob a statesman of the right to make those distinctions between shades of good and evil which are necessary for responsible action in a fallen world. Gandhi was a glowing exception, he did not make the mistake of assuming that it did not matter which side won either of the two world wars. Because his whole political life had been centred upon a struggle for national independence, he knew that in most conflicts it is necessary to take sides, because neutrality is a vote for the aggressor. Nor did he evade the nasty questions which all-out pacifism poses. When asked whether he was prepared to see Jews exterminated by the Nazis, he did not hide behind the claim the whole thing was not really happening – that stories about the extermination of the Jews were a scare conjured up by the armament manufacturers to precipitate a commercially advantageous war. The Jews, he said, ought to commit collective suicide as they did once before in their history at Masada in AD 73. Such a sacrifice would, he believed, arouse the world to Hitler's violence. That is a very odd solution because I cannot see what moral difference there is between doing violence to an enemy and doing violence to oneself – surely both acts should be equally abhorrent to the pacifist? Nevertheless Gandhi faced the unthinkable squarely. He was equally adamant in 1942 when he urged upon the Indian people non-violent resistance against a Japanese invasion, admitting that his way would cost several million lives.

The pacifist has, I think, an optimistic view of human nature. It is to his credit. He believes that even power-mad tyrants are open to rational appeal, that one must think firmly of individuals rather than collectivisms and hope that it is possible to melt the iron curtains of despotism using only the balm of goodwill. He also believes that evil left unchecked will in some mysterious way defeat itself. At its most extreme, this view was held by those pacifists who, with immense courage during the Second World War, insisted that we should allow Hitler to conquer the entire world rather than use force against him, confident that in time Nazism would develop into something different and more benign than the poisonous growth then choking the world. That is a logical position, though it is not one I share, any more than I can bring myself to believe that if minority rule in South Africa, say, is allowed to continue unchallenged it will in due time lead to justice for the blacks – why should it? If whites *sincerely* believe that black rule will mean their very extinction, why would they submit to it voluntarily?

Regrettably, my experience does not allow me to believe that evil left unchecked eventually defeats itself – you either fight it or feed it, and each of these alternatives involves getting your hands dirty. To allow the Nazis to rule the world would have been to connive at evil; but to overthrow them by war was also to traffic in evil. And those were the only alternatives. There was no idealistic middle way. The text for such terrible times as these is not 'He that lives by the sword will perish by it' but 'There is none righteous, not one. . . .'. If that is true then we are in the miserable business of having to judge different forms of evil by marginal percentages. That is what statesmanship is all about underneath the pomp and circumstance – knife-edge judgements that one course of action will be slightly less harmful than another. To canvas a guiltless third way as the pacifist does is to risk irrelevance. I know this – having prayed and pleaded and waited for the whites in Rhodesia to awaken from their sleep and see what terrible things they were doing to their black fellow citizens and neighbours in the name of so-called civilization. Sadly, it was not the murmur of sweet reason but the sound of gunfire which alerted them to the hour of judgement.

So I have found that the demands of political realism have led me to modify my pacifist convictions. Even as I write these words I can imagine the howls of betrayal and comments about the convenient flexibility of the politician's principles. I shall have to bear with fortitude the understandable cries of outrage and merely reply to my critics – have *you* tried running a country on the basis of pacifist principles without qualification or modification, and do you know anyone else who has?

Illusion of Innocence

Is it ever possible to organize political revolutions in which nobody gets hurt? For a long time I thought so, but I failed to take account of two things – the shock which drastic change of any kind causes the human system (though any surgeon could have told me that) and the 'knock-on' effects of all human actions, however well-meant. It would need a philosopher to explain why there is this warp in human existence which has the effect of distorting even our best behaviour. The radical pacifist resolves to secure political and social change solely by taking the kind of actions which would not harm a hair on the head of a single human being and yet he sets in train a series of consequences he would not have wished and probably could not foresee. It has often been pointed out that when the Mahatma Gandhi declared war on the British Raj he chose his weapons with great care so that he would not violate the principle of *satyagraha*. One such weapon was a boycott of imported British cotton – pickets outside clothing stores urged shoppers not to buy the products of English mills. This, felt Gandhi, was a tactic at once effective and yet harmless; the British Government would feel the pinch without anyone getting hurt. In the event, the victims of the cotton boycott were Lancashire children brought to the verge of starvation through the closure of the mills. That sinister 'warp' in events which twisted Gandhi's legitimate actions and did grievous damage was, in this case, a world-wide economic depression. Gandhi was not wrong to have used the boycott weapon, merely naive if he really thought no-one would get hurt as a result.

I myself felt that Sir Harold Wilson was mistaken when in 1965 prior to Rhodesian UDI, he announced that Britain would not use force but implement economic sanctions instead. Some hailed this as a humanitarian gesture. I thought then, and still think now, that Sir Harold's statement was regrettable, not only because it gave Mr Smith all the assurance he needed to go ahead with UDI, but also because thousands in Zimbabwe, black and white, paid with their lives for the British Government's hesitancy. Firm action then, or even the threat of it, could well have forestalled the long, dragging, bloody civil war that resulted. Britain indeed kept her hands unstained by human blood, if that is how Sir Harold's statement is to be interpreted, but she did not thereby do anything to make easier a peaceful settlement of conflict. By discreditably quitting the field she left it for others to do her fighting for her – the freedom fighters of Zimbabwe and their allies in other African states.

Some sympathetic observers of the Southern Africa scene who find violence abhorrent no doubt applauded Sir Harold Wilson's decision to apply sanctions as a civilized alternative to war. But economic sanctions if firmly applied (and I draw a veil over the revelations about breaches of the oil embargo which at least make one wonder how firm Britain really was) are only more humane than war in the sense that starving someone to death is more humane than shooting him. A side-effect of full-blooded sanctions may well be to drive to desperation those who bear the full brunt of them, the poorest and most vulnerable, so that they rise in revolt against their masters. But because such an uprising is likely to be spontaneous and fuelled by hatred and despair rather than the outcome of careful planning, the consequences must be calamitous. Given a country like Zimbabwe where the gap between the haves and the have nots is not only dramatically wide but also represents a racial gulf, economic sanctions, half-heartedly applied, only caused the haves minor inconvenience. Ruthlessly deployed they could have made civil war a real possibility.

Pacifist or non-violent alternatives to force in places where there is a high degree of tension tend to have a detonator effect. Of themselves they are comparatively harmless, just as it is a comparatively harmless thing to strike a match in the dark – unless one happens to be in a confined space permeated by highly explosive gasses. For instance, some urge the use of tactics such as the strike, boycott and picket to paralyse from within the oppressive South African regime. At first sight they seem alternatives infinitely preferable to violent revolution, but only because those who hold such views are ignoring the dynamics of South African society.

South Africa is not, as its supporters like to claim, stable, peaceful and tension-free until disturbed by agitators. On the contrary, it is in a condition of delicately poised equilibrium, with massive forces evenly balanced – State power at full stretch holding in check mass indignation. And when great weights precisely matched hold the beam of a scale horizontal it takes only a feather floating down on this side or the other to destroy the state of balance. Tactics which in some societies would be only feather-light in their impact could well trigger the waves which shake the whole South African system to pieces. That may be what needs to be done, and these tactics may be the most merciful way of doing it. I would only plead that those who in their idealism advocate these allegedly non-violent tactics realize just what they are doing. In trying to avoid the certainty of armed confrontation they are running the risk of sparking off an uncontrolled and uncontrollable explosion. They may be right; each of us must search his conscience in deciding which of these appalling alternatives is the less devilish. What we must not do is underestimate the possible effects of even the least violent forms of revolutionary activity in a society where racial tension is at snapping point. There are some situations so explosive that it is almost an academic question whether an honest error of judgement is morally preferable to an act of deliberate malice. The end result is the same – catastrophe.

I am sometimes accused of a deep and unnecessary pessimism about the prospects for South Africa. Those who upbraid me for being a prophet of doom seem unable to grasp one, simple awful truth – we have run out of alternatives as between violent and non-violent solutions to the South Africa problem. More accurately, the South Africa regime, on its mad roller coaster ride to disaster has passed forever the last of the junction points which might have diverted the thundering juggernaut into a gentler terrain. We are almost at the point where the only question worth agonizing about is not, 'Shall it be by violent or peaceful methods that matters are settled?' but, 'What kind of violence must it be?' The text which is written across the skies of that Bible-loving land is taken from the Book of Chronicles: 'Thus saith the Lord: take what you will; either three years of famine or else three days of the sword of the Lord or else three months' devastation by your foes.' Yet it is not the Almighty who has decreed this terrible destiny but the continuing obduracy of racists who must now soon face the Judgement.

We are told that one of the features of our time is that people have unparalleled freedom of choice in every area of life compared with earlier times. The tragic thing about South Africa is the complete absence of any choices that make sense. What kind of a choice is it between the dreadful and the unthinkable? At the end of the day I fear that the drama can only be brought to its climax in one of two ways – through the selective brutality of terrorism or the impartial horrors of war. And I weep as I write the words.

South Africa's so-called friends frequently exhort the rest of the world to mind its own business and let the people of the Republic work out their own salvation free from outside interference. This is to ignore one of the inescapable facts of life in the realm of international relations. There are no longer any zones of isolation within which what happens to part of mankind is of no interest to the rest. Nor are there areas which the great power blocs can afford to ignore because they are of no strategic significance to them. With the world balanced always on the knife-edge of nuclear war, any country, however small or remote, which is chronically unstable because of explosive internal tensions that cannot be released by constitutional means might be the possible 'trigger' of a holocaust.

Just as nature abhors a vacuum, so great concentrations of political power are drawn like opposing armies to meet across any available no man's land. Near Mfuwe I have watched a pride of lion stalking a herd of zebra. When the stampede begins which of that seething mass of fleeing animals will they chase, I wonder? The answer seems to be that predators have a 'nose' for a sick or weakened beast, and in an instant, select, isolate, chase and kill it. Thus the society riddled with disease is natural prey for international predators. That is why the choices facing South Africa are so bleak.

I am not suggesting that the tactics of violence and those of non-violence are indistinguishable. Nor do I think that since whatever revolutionary action we take must harm *somebody*, it does not matter if we do harm indiscriminately. I seek only to dispel the illusion of innocence, for no fanaticism is so dangerous as that which attaches to the presumption of virtue in the political field. The political innocent who moves cockily into places where hard-bitten political operators fear to tread is like a man taking his dog for a stroll down the fast lane of a motorway, confident that the laws of the universe plus the laws of the road plus the laws of chance will conspire to ensure a safe journey for himself and every other traveller. The resulting carnage is likely to demonstrate that his power to create havoc is out of all proportion to his size and worldly importance. By all means we need those who bring to bear upon Southern

Africa's problems qualities of idealism and courage but they must be yoked in double harness with a healthy scepticism, close observation of human affairs and above all a deep understanding of the dark forces at work in one's own heart. For we ourselves are part of the battlefield on which great issues are being fought out.

Who's Ahead when the Whistle Blows?

When I recall my childhood and early schooling at the mission station in Lubwa, two ghostly sounds echo in my ears – the congregation in the chapel fervently chanting metrical psalms, and a whistle, around which much of my young life seems to have been organized. Everything started and stopped to the sound of that whistle. I do not know what modern educationalists think about these old methods but my schoolmaster believed in developing a fiercely competitive spirit in us – understandable, I suppose, in a Protectorate whose educational system was so inadequate that the chances of an African child getting any schooling at all were not good and of winning a higher education almost infinitesimal. So everything was a race against time, measured by the blowing of that infernal whistle – whether practising shots at goal, picking mealies, collecting berries, getting sums right – whoever had most when the whistle blew was the winner.

I often think of my teacher, the Reverend Maxwell Robertson and his whistle when I am on the receiving end of good advice from my Western friends, and I get a lot of it. But I have noticed that whatever its subject, this advice is frequently offered from the standpoint of those who have got it made, who were ahead when the whistle blew and now want to declare the competition at an end. For example, I am often warned of the danger of the freedom struggle in Southern Africa escalating until the great powers are sucked in and we are on the brink of nuclear disaster. This possibility haunts my dreams, so I agree with such warnings, pausing only to comment that it is the friends who issue the warnings who also have the nuclear devices and therefore whatever the provocation in Southern Africa there cannot be a nuclear war unless for their own reasons they decree there shall be one. Speaking as a citizen of Africa I would insist that there is nothing so great at stake on this continent as to justify the risk of ending the world.

But some of my Western friends are not content with making this strategic point, they want to turn it into a philosophy of non-revolution on the grounds of nuclear risk. They argue that all revolutions must now be ruled out because they are likely to lead to indiscriminate war with the real possibility of a nuclear holocaust. It is that whistle again. Because the superpowers happen to have the Bomb when the whistle is sounded to signal the end of all internal struggles for justice in the poor countries, they can lean on these nations with a sense of moral superiority. It will be all your fault, they warn, if we have to blow the world apart. So on the shoulders of a Southern African freedom fighter battling against great odds for justice and human dignity, there is laid the responsibility for preserving world peace. *He* and his like will answer at the bar of history if someone in Moscow or Washington or Peking decides to put an end to civilization. This is like saying that the lamb being devoured by a leopard is to blame for the leopard's indigestion.

Who's Ahead when the Whistle Blows?

It has always intrigued me that the most passionate calls for restrictions on the spread of nuclear weapons usually come from those powers who have most of them. They always want to blow the whistle whilst they are ahead. I personally would wish to see total nuclear disarmament – nothing less can prevent the terrifying possibilities against which we are always being warned. But I must protest against the arrogant assumption that those powers which already form the nuclear club have the right to freeze its membership on the grounds that they can be trusted with nuclear weapons whereas the people of say, Zambia or Switzerland or Iceland could not.

And what goes for attempts to limit the supply of nuclear weapons to those who already possess them, also goes for revolution in general. I have occasionally in international gatherings been lectured to the effect that the revolutionary struggle of the peoples of Zimbabwe, Namibia and South Africa for justice and freedom is bound to be self-defeating; nothing lasting and worthwhile, I am solemnly told, has ever been achieved by violence. My difficulty about such sermons is that invariably those preaching them are representatives of countries which have not only attained economic and political advantages by force but have, in recent history, demonstrated they are prepared to use a decisive amount of violence, with or without the sanction of international law, to protect the good life they enjoy.

There are undoubtedly sound moral, political and even religious reservations about the justice-through-revolution theory and they must be most carefully weighed, as I have tried to do over the past few years. But as we agonize in torment of spirit about the right thing to do, we ought

71

surely to be spared the sanctimonious moralizing of the great powers who, just as a rich burglar is not a good advertisement for honesty, are hardly shining examples of defenceless virtue.

The 'blow the whistle whilst you're ahead!' philosophy is, at root, pure fascism in its effects. In the deadly power game, those who get ahead and blow the whistle and then distribute amongst themselves the uniforms and symbols of authority, go on to pass laws which validate these symbols and protect what they have managed to carve out for themselves. The losers then find themselves not only confronting superior power, but power vested with the semi-mystical status of authority. Should they wish to argue, they cease to be merely losers, they become rebels. And the dividing line between legitimate and unlawful use of force is neatly drawn, morality meekly following law into the winner's enclosure. So as if by magic, winners and losers are transformed into government and rebels, security forces and guerrillas, policemen and wrongdoers.

There is an element of exaggeration in that description, but it should not prevent the winners of this world from seeing how things look from the other side of the barbed wire. Certainly every effective government, however it gained power, attaches to itself a genuine aura of authority if only because, up to a point, good order is preferable to chaos, strong rule better than anarchy. But that authority becomes contemptible unless it has some basis in a morality superior to that of the ethics of the winner. I suppose the soundest basis is the consent and respect of most of the governed. Where this is lacking, all the impedimenta of statehood, the uniforms and symbols and laws are meaningless, or worse, a licence to commit tyranny.

Who's Ahead when the Whistle Blows?

Sternly moralistic observers of the power struggles in Africa, Asia and Latin America tend to be literal in their interpretation of St Paul's saying that the Powers-that-Be are ordained by God, and they recognize uniforms, military titles and national flags as symbols of that ordination. So security forces represent order keeping at bay chaos personified by barefooted peasants fighting with anything that comes to hand. The matter of deciding where justice lies only becomes urgent when a regime behaves so outrageously that the world can avert its eyes no longer. Even then, one government will give another government the benefit of the doubt for a very long time, unless of course its own interests are directly threatened. Hitler happily pursued his bloody, maniacal way for almost a decade, whilst the rest of the world closed its eyes to what it could not approve. After all, his regime did represent strong, stable government built from the ruins of the Weimar Republic. The nations which were later known as the Allies, like the occupants of a dug-out canoe, observed with interest the crocodile picking off the rest of the fleet. Only when it turned its attention to them did they decide they had better do something about it.

The topsy turvy nature of the freedom struggle in Zimbabwe must have been morally confusing for those who choose sides in any conflict on the basis that Paul's text is the best hope for stability in a jittery world. Mr Ian Smith and his government, for all the trappings of authority they sported, were in fact rebels; traitors who stole a country from its rightful owners (in law) the British. The so-called terrorists were, according to that same law, loyal subjects of the Queen, fighting against her enemies. You might find that hard to believe if you read the version of the conflict regularly offered by large sections of the British press, according to which Mr Smith was a Christian gentleman, who with his white fellow countrymen was struggling to save Rhodesia from the barbarian hordes, who were, of course, the majority of the people. And the British Government, Her Majesty's Government, either by malice or incompetence, helped, through breaches of the oil embargo, to fuel the war-machine of Her Majesty's enemies. Is it really any wonder that the black peoples of Southern Africa have exhausted their capacity to wonder at the hypocrisy and duplicity of the West? Beneath all the bluster and moralizing and cant, one simple, crude lesson seems to be taught by the recent sordid history of Zimbabwe – whites of the world stick together! I hate to think that, but how else can we interpret the evidence?

We Zambians were baffled by the involved logic and the crazy ethics of a British Government which first of all invited us as a nation to accept severe economic hardship in bearing the brunt of sanctions against Rhodesia. This same Government then connived (and that is the kindest word I dare use without doing violence to the truth) at breaches of the oil embargo by companies, one of which it actually owns. This faithful ally then sat back and watched the Rhodesian war machine fuelled by this oil exterminate black freedom fighters who were doing Britain's job for her. And Rhodesian jets, also fuelled by this oil, regularly bombed Britain's ally Zambia whilst the British Government did nothing except wag a finger at Mr Smith and tell him what a naughty boy he was. A naughty boy he assuredly was, but he is also a white boy – that is what our people say – so what is a little matter of treason and murder between kith and kin? This is the message which comes across loud and clear to us mocking our efforts to banish racism from the continent of Africa.

The Smith regime and his supporters both inside Rhodesia and throughout the world were, in the strict sense of the word, fascists. They believed the Rhodesian state had a Divine right to exist, no matter how it came into being and what means had to be used to maintain its existence. They took that country by theft and held it by violence and repression. Questions of justice, legality and morality were swept aside. They believed might makes right, that power is self-justifying and that loyalty to one's own race is everything and excuses the subjugation of fellow-citizens who do not share this mysticism of blood. If that is not fascism, what is? Well, faced with this sort of poisonous doctrine, black Africans had to do some painful rethinking of their own position. If questions of justice, legality and morality *can* be swept aside, it seemed clear that if it was right to use violence to defend such a state, it could not be wrong to use violence to destroy it. So they did.

PART THREE

Peace Myths

There are not many decisions a man or woman will take in
a lifetime that are so momentous as the resolve to stand on
one side or the other of the line which divides pacifists from
non-pacifists. This is not simply a political issue; it affects
our attitudes to virtually every other area of human life.
Like matrimony, it is 'not to be taken in hand lightly and
thoughtlessly but soberly, discreetly and in the fear of
God'. What would in any circumstances be a hard thing to
do is made much worse by the fog of specious arguments
used by misguided advocates of either position to reinforce
their claim upon our loyalty. Wrestling with the serious
ideas is sufficiently taxing upon the mind and spirit without
having to beat off silly notions which swarm about our
heads like angry bees. After all, to kill or allow oneself to be
killed for the wrong reasons is not only wasteful of human
life; it also turns martyrs into fools. If a close examination
of the Gospels could show that Jesus went to the Cross a
deluded or mistaken man, his authority as well as his life
would have been forfeit. The reason for his death must
stand up to close scrutiny by both friends and foes who,
whether or not they thought him right, at least respected
his action as a serious response to a grave problem.

Like most responsible politicians, I am frequently bom-
barded by pamphlets, books and speeches from pacifists and

non-pacifists who either want to win me for their side or, if they feel I have already strayed, seek to lead me back to the fold. Unless they are crackpots, I always listen to these friends with close attention – at least they *care* about great matters of life and death. But I notice that some arguments continually pop up on both sides of the question which need to be put firmly in their place or they will dominate the discussion. The cherished myths are usually demonstrably false, but they are dangerous, not because they are strong but because they are weak. They can be dismissed without too much effort – thus leading to the mistaken impression that the whole case has been disposed of.

For instance, pacifists often assert that wars never settle anything, that they leave behind more problems than they are fought to solve. Now, this is true in one way. When we track down war to its den, we find it is located in the sinful heart of man, so wars will presumably persist for as long as he does. I agree with this analysis. It is borne out by the history books. We read, for instance, how the victorious Allies after the First World War imposed such vengeful restrictions upon the defeated Germany that they made the Second World War inevitable. But to use this as an argument against war is like telling a farmer that it is a waste of time tearing up the weeds in his maize field because more weeds will grow. The point is: in the meantime does he want any maize? War is just like bush-clearing – the moment you stop, the jungle comes back even thicker, but for a little while you can plant and grow a crop in the ground you have won at such terrible cost.

When someone tells me that war never settles anything, I ask him to show me the *kraal* of Shaka Zulu or introduce me to the Governor-General of Portuguese East Africa or tell me how the Third Reich is getting along. That's just the point, retorts my critic, war may bring one tyranny to an end but it will be replaced by another, and he will almost certainly point to those two great bogeys, China and the USSR where, so we are to believe, reigns of terror by the old regime were followed by reigns of terror presided over by those who were once terrorized.

The form of this argument I hear most often comes from the Western press which loves to describe in lurid detail the so-called chaos in black Africa and advises the oppressed people of Southern Africa that they are much better off under their white masters than at the mercy of African tyrants like me. Gullible Western readers are assured that millions of Africans north of the Zambezi are sighing for the good old days of colonialism. This, sadly, is the level at which much of the debate about Southern Africa is conducted in the West. I weary of trying to teach these white lovers of vanished Empire a simple fact of life they have failed to learn from their own history. Even if it were true that for a while the citizens of an African country might find things tougher under a black government than under that of the old white colonialist rulers, most people would rather be dragooned by their own kind than by aliens.

I fear I am laying myself open to misunderstanding in making that point. But I must stick to the truth and let the misrepresentations take care of themselves. I abhor every form of tyranny, whatever the colour of the tyrant's skin, but the difference in Africa between humane white colonialist rule and inhumane black rule is this – one is the result of good coming out of evil, the other, of the good being disfigured by evil. I make this point simply to illustrate the fact that there can be all the difference in the world morally between two systems which at first sight seem very similar, and a war which leads to one being replaced by the other is not necessarily utterly sterile. There is often a terrifying finality about the way wars deal with some issues.

If it is true that wars only settle one set of problems at the price of creating others, could not the same thing also be said about the strategies of peace? When Britain and her allies stood back and allowed Mussolini to devastate Abyssinia in 1935 or appeased Hitler at Munich, just what finality was there about these 'peaceful' solutions to the challenge of tyranny? When Sir Harold Wilson ruled out military intervention against Rhodesia after Mr Smith's declaration of UDI in 1965, how much suffering in the long run did he spare the people of that miserable country?

Without doubt, the strategies of peace are infinitely preferable to those of war if they *work*, but when mankind is confronted by a great evil, if the peaceful way fails, it is not idealism but idiocy to fold one's arms and claim there is absolutely nothing to be done because we all know that war never settles anything. When evil rages, the question of the weapons by which it must be fought is a practical rather than a philosophical one – which options are both effective and economical in human life and resource? It is the classical surgical problem of knowing how to cut deeply enough to root out the poisonous growth without doing mortal damage to the organism.

Man is a very practical animal. He has survived all the threats to his existence by finding workable solutions to perennial problems. He is learning new tricks all the time, but he also keeps a few old ones up his sleeve – they are the ones he has so far found irreplaceable. Tragically, war is one such institution. Man has suffered so greatly in wars throughout recorded time it must be assumed that if there were a more efficient way of achieving whatever end war serves, he would have found and applied it long ago.

The possibility of nuclear extinction may (and ought) to change everything, but it is significant that scientists, military men and economists are now busy working out how best to organize the survival of a *proportion* of the human race. They play what I believe are called nuclear war games to see just how far they dare go with those devilish weapons without destroying the planet. And this means that those of us who confidently assumed that possession of the ultimate weapon must rule war out of the question were wrong. Someone. . . . they. . . . we are exploring ways of combining efficiency – to bomb the enemy into submission – with economy – taking the least possible risk with the survival of the whole human race.

So another dream has faded, that of man entering the nuclear age carrying only an olive branch in his hand, having left his bombs outside this new Garden of Eden. Wars will go on: the experts have decided it is safe for man to continue playing his oldest team game. I do not believe that man is beastly through and through; if wars survive it is because he has found them the most effective way of dealing with some problems. That is a dreadful thing to think, let alone set down on the record, but there is no point in trying to take refuge in illusion. No society throughout history has found a way of abolishing war, so it is pointless arguing that wars never settle anything – as though the moment the argument were put, the truth of it would be obvious. I wish to God it were!

Another pacifist argument identifies war as the disease of a particular political system. So long as there is capitalism/communism/nationalism/colonialism there will be wars. This is an effective way of combining moral indignation with our own political biases. Capitalism is the natural culprit of the left-winger. Those ogres, the armament manufacturers, are the only ones who make a profit from wars – so the propaganda blurb runs. And it is quite untrue; whole societies may benefit economically as a result of war. I recall my surprise when I read an article in *The Economist* written by a British Chancellor of the Exchequer explaining why the British economy was lagging behind that of Germany. The main reason, he pointed out, is that Germany not only lost the war but was so devastated that she had to start from scratch building up her industry again. Britain, on the other hand, survived the war with her economy largely intact and so moved into the post-war world with old-fashioned equipment. I was puzzled by this argument because it seemed so topsy turvy to my mind, but I have no reason to doubt its truth. The Second World War transformed the face of the continent of Africa, and so its effect upon those nations who were the major combatants must have been immense. Nor was it only capitalist societies whose economies were shaken and rebuilt as a result of war – *The Economist* article instanced the USSR as a nation which was stagnating during the 1930s but made great advances following 1945.

The record of the communist bloc hardly bears out the contention of the left-wing pacifist that war is a capitalist phenomenon. These states have done their share of fighting since 1945, either amongst themselves or standing behind other nations such as Korea and Vietnam. Whatever the differences between capitalism and communism, one thing they seem to have in common is a tendency to engage in war-making. Nor, I must confess to my shame, has independent Africa during its short and stormy history avoided the curse of war. Driving out the colonialists has not meant an end to armed conflict as some optimists hoped. Be it said, most of the wars which rocked the continent in the past few years have been the consequence of the policies of colonial powers – either their direct interference in the internal affairs of African states or the effect of those territorial boundaries they imposed with such lack of respect for African traditional history. Still, colonialism and nationalism stand in the dock together on the charge of incitement to war.

War is not the characteristic disease of one particular political system but of one particular being, man, who contrary to what many pacifists believe, is prepared to take up arms with terrifying eagerness. It is a popular belief that warlike leaders stir up their peaceful followers to hate and fight some chosen enemy. In fact, some leaders have been thrown out of office because they tried to hold in check the people's enthusiasm for war.

The impulse to war bridges the generation gap and the class barrier. A central figure in all national histories is the warrior-hero who does epic deeds of bravery on the battlefield and helps save the nation. Whenever I pay my somewhat infrequent trips to London, I am intrigued by the number of monuments and statues to military heroes which occupy prominent places at the heart of the capital. There are lots of these statues around Westminster from whose Parliament I regularly receive good advice to the effect that there is no way forward in Southern Africa through the use of force. War, these much-decorated war veterans tell me, is self-defeating and degrading and will never solve anything. The day the British Secretary for Defence stands up in the House of Commons and announces that not one penny will be spent on the armed forces in the ensuing year I will believe it all. Meanwhile, they must forgive me for harbouring the suspicion they mean that war *against whites* is degrading – as when a boy strikes back at the headmaster instead of taking his birching like a man.

It is crying for the moon to imagine that by changing the political system or switching the balance of power between generations or races we can irradicate war. The argument fails because the hearer, if he has any self-insight, rejects it at the level of his heart rather than his head. He *knows* that deep within him are attitudes and feelings which will incite to violence whatever political system tries to contain them.

Nor is it enough for the pacifist to claim that non-violence is an alternative policy to war. Non-violence is not a policy at all. It is the refusal to accept one specific policy, force, as a solution to certain problems. The disciple of non-violence is announcing that he will not go up that road which leads to the battlefield, and this can be a costly and courageous thing to do. But his decision has no bearing at all on the issues which are being fought out on the battlefield. It is what the pacifist does next that counts. Only then can he be taken seriously because he is beginning to form an alternative policy rather than express his abhorrence of the one which exists. If I state the obvious, it is because I am frequently urged to accept 'non-violence' as a solution to the immensely complex problems of Southern Africa. But what is this 'non-violence'? Is it a magic password like 'Abracadabra!'? 'Non-violence' is no more a solution to the tragic mess in Southern Africa than 'non-surgery' is a cure for a seriously ill patient. It merely tells us that the doctor is choosing not to exercise one amongst a dozen options. But it is what he does next that will seal the patient's fate.

When the pacifist starts to spell out the second step, his sharp convictions become somewhat vague. I have before me as I write a pamphlet published in 1978 by the Fellowship of Reconciliation called *War Under Judgement* written by Mr Alan Litherland. It is a most moving and eloquent indictment of war, and I turned anxiously to the chapter headed 'Alternatives to Armed Force' to see what I might learn. The author deals with Soviet Russia in one paragraph, Zimbabwe in three and Northern Ireland in four. I salute him for taking on challenges from which some of the most prominent politicians of our time shrink. Had more citizens of Britain and elsewhere shown the same degree of concern as the author we might not have had to go to war in Southern Africa. But in the brief paragraph about Zimbabwe I am offered suggestions about gestures and symbolic actions which might have some propaganda value but nowhere is there a trace of anything one might call the raw material of policy. I am of course criticizing one brief paragraph in a very short book. But this is just the problem – I have never yet come across a *big* book about Southern Africa in which the strategies of non-violence are dealt with in such detail that they cease to define the attitudes of dedicated individuals and become credible policies for determining the crucial issues of power and justice.

I am afraid this confirms my view that non-violence is an expression of moral outrage and a personal declaration of intent but does not offer the raw stuff of political policies. Of course, the best way pacifists can refute that statement is not to engage in endless debate about the principle but produce the blueprint by means of which we may smash the iron regime of South Africa and liberate her peoples without using force. That is the test case, that is the issue which will overshadow my nation and most others in independent Africa for the next decades.

It is significant that the Bhuddists in Vietnam whose hatred of violence has very deep spiritual roots were unable to launch an effection non-violence movement during the war in South-East Asia. Individual monks burned themselves alive, others went to gaol and there were Bhuddists in the government who provided some moderating influence, but at no point were the devotees of that great and ancient faith able to create a ground swell of popular opinion in favour of non-violence. Some might say this was because non-violence demands a degree of courage and sacrifice beyond the capacity of most people. A more likely reason is that the ordinary Vietnamese recognized that just stopping the war would leave all the major issues unresolved. Where would the balance of power be struck between the overwhelming US military presence, the North Vietnamese forces and the popular liberation front, the Viet Cong? The result of an unlikely conversion to non-violence must be paralysis rather than peace because the hard questions are left hanging in the air. Once a war of liberation has begun, it must be fought through to a verdict – anything short of that must leave the *status quo* with the advantage and the freedom forces, because they are invariably less well equipped, will pay a heavy price for little return.

Cries of 'Stop the War now!' have a strong emotional appeal whatever the nature of the conflict which evokes them. But unless we are to assume that nations go to war because they have nothing better to do with their time and substance, the peace slogan is an invitation to short-circuit the grievous differences which give rise to war in the first place. One of the functions of war – and I do not find it pleasant to discuss the subject in this cold and detached way – is to redefine power relationships which have become blurred; to test out how far the writ of disputing parties really runs. For choice, all statesmen in their right minds would do these things by a process of negotiation and diplomacy, and for most of the time, thank God, that is how the world rubs along. But a nation which forfeits moral authority by restricting or denying the human rights of its people or of other people over whom it exercises sovereignty is distorting the evolving shape of an enlightened world community. And should this defiance lead to war, it is pointless demanding that the war be stopped for humanitarian reasons if the crucial issue remains non-negotiable.

I am personally most vulnerable to the charge that in supporting the freedom struggle I am breaking Jesus's second great commandment that I must love my neighbour as myself. For many Christian pacifists this is the clinching argument in support of their case. How is it possible to reconcile love for one's neighbour with killing him? And Jesus's definition of the neighbour – one whose need I can supply wherever he may be on the face of the earth – does not leave me much room for picking and choosing those for whom I bear some responsibility. So those young white Rhodesian lads who flew their jets across my country and bombed refugee camps are my neighbours; so are the black Selous Scouts who raided remote, defenceless Zambian villages, leaving behind them a trail of terror and destruction; so are all those politicians in Southern Africa committed to repellent doctrines of racial superiority. Yes, they too are my neighbours.

Now, can I reconcile love for my neighbour with killing him? No, I cannot, and it is a waste of time trying to prove otherwise. But I would ask those who impale me upon this cross a simple question which in no way offers my conscience ease but must surely be placed in the balance on the other side: can I reconcile love for my neighbour with watching him from a distance being brutalized and tormented and reduced to the level of an animal *and do nothing about it?* And if what I actually do in no way eases his burden, how can my action be an expression of that strong thing Jesus called love? It is sentimentality which would have me wringing my hands helplessly and tut-tutting the awfulness of it all; it is love that runs terrible risks to help free my brothers and sisters so they may realize their Divine destiny.

Words frighten me because of the ease with which they can be woven into a pretty tapestry that hides ugly truths. So I offer only this thought about the absurdity of trying to love my neighbour whilst in the act of using violence against him. As I understand it, love is between *people*. Any system which treats some members as superhuman and others as subhuman renders love between the two impossible. Hence, if it is necessary to raise up the oppressed to the dignity of persons in order that they may love their neighbours, so by the same token, those who act as though they are superhuman, the oppressors, must be cast down to make it possible for them to reciprocate their neighbour's love. Now, it is not hard to show that liberating the oppressed by the use of force is an act of love, but can our minds grasp the unthinkable idea that the oppressors also need to be re-humanized possibly by the use of force which destroys their claim to be superhuman?

There are two ways of robbing men of their humanity – to reduce them to the level of animals or magnify them to the status of devils. Both conditions are an affront to God. So, to make love possible they must each revert to full humanity, neither more nor less. If it is right to use force on behalf of the oppressed to give them back their humanity, why is it wrong to use force against the oppressor to restore him to true humanity also and make him capable of love?

This line of argument does not get to grips with the terrible possibility that in the act of showing love to the oppressed by using force to free him I may also kill the oppressor. How is the oppressor's capacity to love restored if his very life is forfeited? I do not know – the philosophers and theologians may debate the principle at length whilst we political leaders have to make the awful decisions which rob people of their lives. I think it comes down to this. You have no option but to be a pacifist if you believe that the worst thing you can do to a man is kill him. But you may think that there is something worse you can do to him – connive at the business of allowing him to become a real devil as he robs others of their humanity and defaces the image of God in them. And to do that you need do absolutely nothing – just fold your arms, shake your head in despair and watch him take himself and his victim to hell. Either way, the choice is terrible, and there is a point beyond which the two positions cannot be reconciled by logic, only by penitence.

Yes, I confess that my love for the oppressed may be at odds with my love for the oppressor. By using force I am making an impossible choice, just as the pacifist by refusing to use force is also making an impossible choice. How can I match my guilt against his? Only by acknowledging that we are united in the fellowship of suffering and the solidarity of guilt – that was the phrase used by the German Church at the time of Hitler to unite those who felt that Hitler must be overthrown if necessary by assassination and those who believed that such an option was not open to the Christian.

War Myths

It is not only on the pacifist side of the debate about violence that somewhat shaky arguments fly around. Non-pacifists also have certain favourite lines of attack, certain houses of illusion in which they hide, certain demons which possess them. This whole debate is in danger of becoming a kind of ritual war dance where the moment one warrior stamps his foot that is the signal for his adversary to raise his spear and so on. We would all benefit by importing into the discussion ideas which do not fall off the tip of our tongues quite so smoothly; ideas we have to struggle to put into words because they are unfamiliar or even only half-formed but have something of the truth in them.

High on the list of jaded ideas which are candidates for a long holiday is the fashionable tendency to idealize revolution and give it a flavour of romance and drama. We politi-

cians must take our share of blame for corrupting the term
to mean something less drastic than it ought to be and
something less awful than it really is. We talk about things
and policies and events as being 'revolutionary' when we
mean they are different from what has gone before.
'Revolutionary' is a big word we often use to state the
obvious truth that things are changing and we would be
wise to change with them. We easily slip into the error of
thinking that revolutions are truly heroic episodes in
human history. This is because our memories are patchy
and distance smooths rough contours – the surface of the
moon looks as polished as a billiard ball from the earth. Additionally, it is usually the victor's account of the battle
which is believed and he is almost certain to point out what
a splendid thing the revolution was.

In case anyone should think I am a recent convert to this
sceptical view about the nature of revolutions, I dug out of
my files the report of a speech I made on the eve of
Zambia's independence in 1964 at the sacred site of our
nation and party, Mulungushi. According to the official
record of the conference, I said this to the delegates:
'Fellow citizens, this has been a hard-won struggle, and I
ask you not to get confused by believing in the American
Revolution, Russian Revolution, Chinese Revolution or
British Revolution. I personally do not believe in such
'ions' and 'isms' other than Zambianism which I would
define simply as the service of man by man by the protection of all that is good in the Zambian way of life'. I well
recall my motive in inserting that passage in my speech. I
detected a tendency on the part of some of our jubilant
party officials to begin glorifying what had been a grim
struggle. Others were disposed to class the modest changes

in Zambia at the point of independence with those world-shaking events which brought the superpowers to birth. The people had to understand that they must rely on their own efforts to achieve salvation and not look admiringly over their shoulders at distant nations and far off times. Even then, when I was a fledgling Head of State, it seemed to me dangerous nonsense to use loosely that explosive term 'revolution' or to draw over-simplified conclusions from the great revolutions of the twentieth century.

When we use words like 'revolution' loosely, it is more than our use of language which suffers. Awful words should be reserved for awful things, otherwise we end up using polite words for terrible things – as when the Americans talked of 'pacifying' Vietnamese villages when they meant razing them to the ground, or the ex-Rhodesian Government described as 'security forces' the bands of licensed killers in uniform who tortured and murdered harmless African villagers. Conversely, because of deliberate tampering with labels, loyal Zimbabwean guerrillas fighting to free their own country became 'terrorists' and virtually anyone in South Africa, whatever his colour, who dares to criticize the government, is condemned as a 'communist' and treated accordingly.

No playing about with words can disguise the hideous reality of revolutions. Changes in the power structure of a country so drastic as to justify being called revolutionary can rarely be achieved without widespread suffering. We in Zambia still remember the chaos on our borders in the Congo in 1960 when certain European interests with a greedy eye on that nation's copper tried to tear the Katanga free from the rest of the Republic of Zaire. Revolution and counter-revolution ravaged that nation not once but twice, dragging in the United Nations Organisation and putting the great powers at odds as they backed one faction against the others. And it would be needlessly harrowing to enumerate the gigantic cost in lives and property of better known revolutions, successful or not, that have shaken the African continent in recent years, let alone elsewhere.

I must be honest – there are times when revolutions are a tragic necessity because the extension of human rights to large numbers of oppressed citizens can be achieved in no other way. But I deplore the habit of giving the term a flavour of moral approval as though by definition all revolutions must be good. Indeed, revolution has become the intellectually acceptable form of modern war. To call any large-scale conflict revolution and identify one side as the revolutionaries is enough to win the sympathy and support of well-meaning people who warm to the sound of the word but are unable to make tough political judgements about the issue. And, of course, the combination of 'left-wing' and 'revolution' is a double pedigree.

Need one point out that some of the most effective revolutions of this century have not placed left-wing regimes in power nor have they led to a greater spread of justice throughout the system? The Spanish Civil War could be called a revolutionary struggle but it led to a repressive Fascist regime under General Franco; the Nazi takeover from the Weimar Republic, though technically accomplished through the ballot box, was revolutionary in its effects. Were these revolutions a 'good thing'? I make the point simply to show that revolutions are no more immune from moral judgement than any other form of conflict, and it is no answer to the pacifist's case to label a war revolutionary as though this sanctified the violence which resulted.

The Riddle of Violence

I have been looking up the text of the historical document which sets out the conditions for what is called the Just War. I read somewhere that a modern variant of this old theological idea and called the doctrine of the Just Revolution has been found helpful by some political philosophers concerned about violence. I was anxious to try it out for myself. The six conditions which must be met if a war is to be considered just are:

1 It must be declared by legitimate authority

2 It must be fought for a just cause

3 It must be fought as a last resort

4 It must have just goals

5 It must be fought by moderate means

6 It must have a reasonable chance of success

Throughout Christian history, this code must have done much to limit suffering and contain the worst effects of war. But I have studied it carefully and must confess it gives me a few headaches. I fear that non-pacifists who say that provided combatants stick to these rules they have a complete answer to the pacifist's case are claiming more than I would care to.

One problem is that it is easy to say 'Amen!' to each of the six conditions whilst in practice reducing them to one – a just war is one fought by my side and an unjust war is one fought by yours. That is unforgivable cynicism on my part but there is just this much truth in the parody – once we have decided which side we are on (and we are usually *born* into that) it can be taken for granted that we will meet all six conditions during any conflict in which we get embroiled. Why? Because it is my observation that no one ever does what he believes is wrong.

Even if what he is doing is condemned according to the laws of God and man, he will still convince himself that he is justified on this occasion in making an exception of himself – and by extension, of his nation. Of course one must salute courageous conscientious objectors who refuse to endorse their country's policies and actions in time of war. But most citizens, swept along on patriotic hysteria, know only one moral imperative – this war must be won! Our lives, our property, our children's future, our freedom depend upon it! So we will make those rules fit somehow.

An illustration might help. I find it useful always to try to see things from my opponent's angle when I wish to predict his likely reaction to any course of action I might take. Hence, I imagined myself Propaganda Minister in what was once Mr Ian Smith's Government having to answer allegations that the regime had violated the rules of civilized behaviour according to the doctrine of the Just War. Let's look at those conditions again:

1 *Legitimate Authority?* 'Legitimate' means approved by the law of the land – Rhodesia. If my government is not, who else is? We have a parliament, judges, police, armed forces and regular elections. We are not recognized by a number of nations, but neither was the government of the People's Republic of China for many years, and who doubts it had 'legitimate authority'?

2 *A Just Cause?* The preservation of Christian civilization against the threat of international communism.

3 *Last Resort?* How many reports and conferences have there been? How many appeals have we made to the terrorists to give themselves up? How long must we put up with aggression?

4 *Just Goals*? We seek the advancement of the African people at a pace related to their state of civilization and the protection of the lives and property of white settlers who built this country.

5 *Moderate Means*? Our security forces are highly disciplined and use normal weapons of the kind Britain used against communist terrorists in Malaya. Our bombing raids on Zambia have been carried out with pinpoint accuracy to kill only terrorists and avoid civilians.

6 *Reasonable Chance of Success*? Our senior officers fought alongside the British in the Second World War; we are more than a match for undisciplined savages. We defeated them in the Matabele War in 1897, and we will do it again.

That case, though laughable to me, would be congenial to the average *Daily Telegraph* reader and it was strong enough to convince those white Rhodesians who wanted to believe it that their cause was just. After all, if they were taken in by their own government's propaganda they must have been convinced they were fighting for survival, and that is the kind of struggle which conforms to a much older code than the doctrine of the Just War – the law of the jungle.

This is the trouble with the theory of the Just War. Most regimes in this world who go to war do not give a damn whether or not their cause is just, they intend to win anyway, whilst those regimes which for whatever reason take note of the doctrine of the Just War have little difficulty in adapting it to fit their circumstances.

How easily cynicism takes possession of our souls! I did not intend to ridicule the doctrine of the Just War nor laugh at those brave theologians and moralists who down the centuries have tried to tame the wild beast of war and bring it under some sort of rational control. I am just afraid that we may make a virtue out of necessity and rob violence of its horror by arguing that provided we stick to a set of rules – those of the Just War or some other – we can at least make violence tolerable. Violence is not and cannot be tolerable! When we resort to violence we have been pushed through sheer despair to the very edge of the frontier which divides man from the beasts. And we must never for a moment forget it, or try to disinfect violence by pouring over it a balm of sweet-scented theology. By all means let there be rules such as those of the Just War or the Geneva Convention so that once battle has been joined some semblance of humanity may be retained, but they must not be used like the small print on a driving licence – so long as you observe these conditions you may bowl along the road at the wheel of car with an easy conscience.

Violence used in the course of a people's war of liberation is not something romantic – it is a cry of despair from the oppressed who can see no other way out. I know that Christians are not supposed to give way to despair, but I think it is less than helpful to tell people whose every day is a living hell that they must remain hopeful because somehow, somewhere, sometime, they will be liberated provided they do not fall into the temptation of using violence. That kind of good Western advice, coming from those who already have freedom and prosperity is an insult to people whose daily lives are a torment and who face every dawn with dread.

The myth-makers of war who are anxious to demonstrate that sometimes violence, far from being a terrible necessity, can be an act of idealism, usually do so by trying to separate the violence itself from the feelings which accompany it. The sort of thing they say is that if we must kill then it is important to do so in the right spirit. There must be no vengefulness, no hatred in our hearts, only love for our neighbour as we seek to annihilate him. I felt myself sliding into that quicksand earlier when I was stating the case for using violence against an oppressor who thinks himself superhuman in order that he might love his oppressed neighbour. It is understandable that we human beings always want to find a moral basis even for the things we have to do out of utter necessity. It seems outrageous to say simply, 'Whether it was right or wrong, I had to do it!' I suppose the underlying assumption of such a remark is that we are puppets on a string rather than free children of God – and this any Christian must reject. Yet it might be more honest to confess the desperate necessity that drives us rather than try to defend a moral absurdity – that we are blasting, maiming, burning, disfiguring someone without any hatred in our hearts. What then, in God's name, *is* in our hearts when we do such things?

An eminent British theologian, Professor J. G. Davies in an important and helpful book (*Christians, Politics and Violent Revolution*, SCM, London, 1976) comments that 'it is possible to kill without malice or spirit of vengefulness' and he goes on, 'No Christian can endorse the sentiments of Che Guevara when he upholds "hatred as a factor in struggle; intransigent hatred for the enemy, which impels one to exceed the natural limitations of the human being and transforms him into an effective, violent, selective and cold killing machine" '. The idea of killing without malice may have been a psychological possibility in the days when tribal clansmen or medieval knights met in hand to hand combat to prove some great point and the winner finished off the loser with tears in his eyes. But I shall never forget that picture which must have appeared in almost every newspaper in the world of a little Vietnamese girl, naked and stumbling in terror down the road, being roasted alive with napalm after the Americans had bombed a place called Trang Bang in 1972. Now this is a ghastly thing to say, but if whoever did that was not motivated by 'malice or spirit of vengefulness', if he really believed he was acting with love in his heart towards that child, then we are all in the madhouse. If the hearts of airmen were filled with a hatred for all things British or German when they bombed Coventry or Dresden flat then at least they were sinful human beings capable of repentance and redemption, but if they destroyed whole cities 'without malice or the spirit of vengefulness' – as unfeelingly as a farmer flattening an ant hill with a hoe – then what sort of empty space was in their hearts?

There is, I fear, a moral and psychological realism about those words of Che Guevara. They are the sentiments of an intelligent and sensitive freedom fighter having to get up the strength to take the lives of others by drinking at the well of darkness. I neither defend him, because I cannot, nor will I attack him because I have no personal experience of the conditions under which the people lived whom he was fighting to liberate. But I do have personal experience of the terrible anger which overtakes the humanist as he sees his brothers and sisters brutalized and humiliated. I remember when I was a small child, my sainted father, beside himself with fury, beating his clenched fist on the table of our little house to the amazement of three white missionaries who had come to berate him for preaching that morning against racial segregation on the mission station. Admittedly he was taking his anger out on an object rather than a person, but I wonder what his reaction might have been had he lived to see racism carried to the lengths of a cold-blooded attempt to wipe whole peoples off the face of the earth?

Public opinion in America was scandalized in the 1960s when black leaders such as Rap Brown and Stokely Carmichael, despairing of the struggle to get equal rights for their people by peaceful means, began to preach hatred against the whites. Phrases such as 'We hate the whites because they have always hated us' and 'The white exploits people so he must be crushed!' and the famous 'Violence is as American as cherry pie!' may not have been very noble sentiments but they were forced out of the mouths of despairing human beings in torment about the fate of their brothers and sisters. On the other hand, the self-righteous whites who expressed horror and outrage at these barbaric opinions were at the same time bombing and blasting Vietnam out of existence. Not out of hatred for the yellow man, we were assured, indeed out of love for him – to free him from the oppression of his own kind, the Viet Cong, so that he might continue to have the American giant, his great ally, sit upon his back and crush him to the ground. Neither expression of violence was particularly admirable. The difference is that the American black was acknowledging frankly that his violent feelings were fuelled by hatred whereas the American white was deluding himself that his military massacre of Vietnam was being done out of love for the people of that land.

The frank expression of hatred on the part of those who embrace violence in desperation has this to commend it – at least it ought to make the ones who have evoked such hatred realize what a terrible thing they have done. Not only have they stolen another human being's freedom and dignity, they have turned him into a devil and therefore wiped out his humanity as well. In contrast, those who resort to violence with calm hearts and call their indifference love, have no sense of right and wrong whatsoever. To hate someone is at least to react to the *person* in him even in the act of hurting him. To hurt someone and feel nothing is to treat the victim as an object, just like the table my father pounded in Lubwa all those years ago.

The person who feels the horrible necessity of using violence in pursuit of justice is boxed in by enough dilemmas without anyone adding to his confusion through speaking approvingly of something called 'pure' or 'innocent' violence. It is easier to milk an angry mamba of venom than separate an act of violence from the strong feelings that motivate it. To talk about killing without malice or hurting someone out of love for him is to reduce man to the status of a non-moral being by implying that he may do terrible things to a fellow human being without bringing down upon himself any moral judgement. This is no answer to the pacifist's case; in fact, it strengthens it because the pacifist insists that to indulge in violence for whatever motive is to reduce oneself to a level lower than the beasts. But more important, those who feel compelled to use violence even for noble ends must not have it made easier for them to deaden their consciences and get rid of their sense of guilt, otherwise they will end up killing for pleasure. Whoever is driven to harm another human being is in need not of vindication but of forgiveness.

There is another line of thought I have come increasingly

to distrust as a justification of violence. In fact, it is not so much an argument as an assumption and I personally find it hard to cope with because it puts me on a knife-edge. It can be described as the conviction that one group or race or class, because history has given it a bad time, can find more excuse than others to use violence to change things for the better. It will be obvious why I as a black man from a long suppressed people engaged in a war of liberation find this a very sensitive issue. I know what my people have suffered; I know what it is like to be judged by the colour of my skin; I have known great poverty and felt hunger in my belly and the demons of envy rising in my heart. I know what injustice and oppression do to the soul of man. So it is a real temptation to go one stage further and claim that my race has gone through so much that its members can be excused for doing almost anything to tip the scales of the balance nearer a just centre point.

We must at all costs avoid double standards, however much some of us may feel we have already paid in advance the bill for any sins we may commit in the course of trying to set things to rights. I have always refused to play with words and make some clever distinction between 'force' and 'violence' – as though the state in killing the rebel is doing something *basically* different from the rebel who kills a soldier. Equally, I do not think that black violence is of a different order from white violence. We must apply the same stringent standards of judgement to each, otherwise we are simply perpetuating the very racism we claim to be using force to smash. This is not a point that needs labouring. We black men and women who are now coming into our own at last as free and responsible sons and daughters of God ought not to ask for special treatment because of our tough past. I weary of the whining of some of my fellow politicians who want to blame the colonial past for everything from the state of the economy to the state of the weather. They remind me of lawyers pleading that their clients in the dock ought to get lenient treatment because they came from bad homes, never had any schooling and fell on their heads as children, which made them a little silly. We are not invalids, mentally or physically, nor are we infants or madmen. There is no hope for Africa until we stop making excuses for ourselves and take the sternest moral and spiritual tests without flinching, on our merits as human beings, expecting neither more nor less than a fair deal from the rest of the world.

But we cannot at one and the same time demand the world stop judging us according to racial categories and then take refuge in those same categories when we are driven to desperation. There is not a special kind of violence called 'black' violence which is exempt from moral judgement because the black man from time immemorial has suffered dumbly under persecution and oppression without lifting his voice or his fist. Certainly, the terrible anger of the long-subject races is understandable and easily explained. If you treat someone for long enough like a dog, it is not hard to understand why he is finally goaded into biting you. So if you oppress the poor, rob them of their dignity, exploit their labour and condemn them and their families to lives of misery, you ought not to be surprised if they eventually give way to an awful anger and tear you and your oppressive class to pieces. But the fact that something is perfectly understandable does not necessarily make it right.

Remember how the Jews in the Old Testament believed they were the chosen people? So they were, but God sent great prophets such as Isaiah and Jeremiah to make it clear that being chosen excused the Jews nothing and indeed laid extra responsibilities upon them. We must therefore lay to rest the notion that there is such a thing as a chosen people or chosen race or chosen class which is excused some of the duties that fall to the whole of humanity. And may I add, with particular reference to Zambia and other parts of Africa, we must also get away from any belief in a chosen tribe? I do not believe that God notices these badges and marks by which we set such store – colour, class, sex or tribal scars. He judges all humanity by quite different standards, and I find it hard to believe that any of the reasons which we offer to justify our less noble actions will make much sense to him.

My point is that I have the right to be judged as a human being, just that. I do not plead the fact that I am black as a justification for my supporting the freedom struggle in Southern Africa. If what I am doing is wrong, then my being black will not and should not save me. If what I am doing is right then my being black does not clothe it with any special merit. I stand before God and my brothers and sisters throughout the world as a free, responsible, adult human being and I do not wish questions about my colour or my past or my people's misery to cloud humanity's judgement of what I do.

I enter only this special plea for some kind of discrimination to be made in judging those who do acts of violence. The rich and powerful have a wide variety of weapons at their disposal which are denied to the poor. The violence of the underdog is strident, crude and obvious. The violence of the top-dog is often subtle and invisible. It spans a range which takes in international economic pressures, control of the media, manipulation of the educational system and psychological conditioning, as well as the more visible strong-arm methods.

It is this gigantic spider's web of interlocking systems that the poor and the black and the helpless are up against. So they have the right to ask that the world is alert to the secret violence which is exerted against them long before they actually retaliate in anger. When the first stone is thrown and the original barricade is stormed that is not the primary move in the game. The truth is not so simple as the usual propaganda ploy tries to suggest – that black or communist or anarchist or nationalist or tribal agitators are disturbing an otherwise peaceful society. The peace was broken long before the first signs of disturbance reached the surface. The underdog demands only this special consideration from the judges in the tribunal at which his desperate actions are weighed – not that he be given any favoured treatment because he is black or poor or voiceless, but that the true magnitude of the forms of violence which can be applied against him because he is black and poor and voiceless be taken fully into account.

Such an unflinching assessment would have two effects upon the debate about violence. On the one hand, the black freedom fighter would not be able to short-circuit the pacifist's arguments because he is black or poor or whatever other special circumstance he tries to offer in mitigation of his actions. On the other hand, the pacifist could just find himself having to redefine violence as he discovers that some of the strategies he has sanctified as non-violent are revealed to be very destructive when used with the blessing of the Establishment against the powerless. For the pacifist should be in no doubt that if he does invent an effective tactic of passive resistance, the Establishment will take it over and use it for its own purposes.

All Africans are great gardeners – Presidents and peasants scratch away at the soil trying to win a little something for the table and cooking pot. It is not so much a hobby as an instinct. Bred into us is the confidence that whatever blows fate may deal us we and our families will survive so long as we have the strength to lift a hoe. But combined with that confidence is a sense of dependence – the sun, the rains and the harvest cannot be hurried. Nature which blesses us one year may curse us the next, so we are not given to easy optimism. We know from hard experience that Africa always wins. We can clear some ground, plant our crops and build our cities, but the bush always comes back. So we have learned to distrust 'final solutions' to anything, and so we are resistant to that cruellest of all the myths of war – the assertion that after this final battle we can beat our swords into ploughshares because they will be of no further use to us except as museum trophies. 'A War to end all Wars!' – that was the slogan which rang in the ears of those marching men on the way to the trenches in 1914. What would they have thought had they known their sons were destined to make that same journey again in 1939?

War simplifies everything. When a nation goes to war all normal business is suspended, political parties declare a truce, the economy is geared to war production, labour disputes are banned and people's lives are turned upside down. The value of everything from a pound of butter to a human life is altered. War is like taking a knife to a tangled ball of string – one slash and all the hours of patient unravelling become unnecessary, until you have to join all the ends together again! It is such an effective solution to the problem of the knotted string because everything changes before your very eyes whereas all that fiddling around with knots does not seem to get anywhere. This dramatic effect of war, together with the way it sucks every aspect of a nation's life into its humming machinery, has given rise to a hope, born out of extremity, that it all need never happen again. Here is truly a final solution.

History gives the lie to this optimism, but most people do not learn from history – politicians least of all, if my experience is anything to go by. Because war is so dramatically effective in changing things, because it appeals to emotions both good and bad which are easily aroused – patriotism and courage, impatience and aggression – and because the alternatives to war seem in comparison so inconclusive, what was intended as the last resort is always in danger of becoming the first resort.

And what applies to war also takes in revolution. Revolution can never be anything other than a *temporary* solution to the problem of justice. That I would wish to emphasize as strongly as I can. Those who choose this way must rid their minds of any illusion that once the tyrant has been overthrown, a thousand years of peace will follow. Somewhere, unnoticed, someone – a child perhaps – is beginning to show the first signs of strange qualities which may one day establish him as a tyrant, or else today's liberators are so intoxicated by the rich wine of power that they become tomorrow's oppressors. It has happened before; it happens all the time.

I write these words during a brief holiday on my family's farm near Chinsali. I watch the villagers going about the traditional system of millet cultivation known as *icitimene*. First, there is *ukutema* – the cutting down or stumping of the trees and dense undergrowth that has grown up during the previous rainy season. Then this brushwood is piled up and burned until it is reduced to an ash rich in nutrients. The soil beneath is also scorched and the lumps broken up by the heat into a powder which makes excellent seedbed. *Ukutema* – shearing the trees of their branches – is a highly skilled occupation. Young men swarm up the tree trunks, hanging on by their hands and pressing with their naked feet until they are amongst the branches which they then hack down. It is a very dangerous business which our young people turn into a sport. When the ground has been cleared, the crop grown and harvested and the rains are over, the people who follow this traditional way move on to another part of the bush and the whole process begins again.

Because such a method of cultivation takes a heavy toll of our trees we are encouraging our people to try other systems of agriculture. But – and this is the point – I notice as I stroll around my farm that even in these tree-cleared areas, recently scorched black by the charcoal burners, green and yellow shoots are already thrusting their way upwards towards the sun again. Africa is reclaiming the bush. It will not be too long before the young men have to climb the strong trees into which those weak shoots will grow. And what has been, will be again.

The *icitimene* system strikes me as an excellent parable. Every detail means something to me – the scorched earth symbolizes the devastation of war, the young men taking their lives in their hands as they enthusiastically cut down the old trees, remind me of the idealism and vigour of the revolutionaries, keen to get rid of deadwood and lay the seedbed of a new society. But it is those young shoots pushing their way out of the burned earth that speak a word of warning. 'Nothing is forever!' they say, 'It will all have to happen again, the cutting down and the burning and raking over of cold ashes to prepare the ground for a new beginning. Let the fruits of the harvest strengthen you for the next round of a battle which will never end'.

The final battle, according to the Bible, is Armageddon, and that will be followed not by a just and peaceful society but by the Last Judgement. I am not arguing that revolution must under all circumstances be ruled out of court because it cannot promise a permanent end to all forms of injustice, but I am saying it is pointless trying to convince pacifists, some of whom have seen not one but two world wars, that the successful outcome of a revolutionary struggle in Southern Africa will usher in Utopia. They will not believe it and we should be fools to imagine there is something unique about our freedom struggle which must make it the war to end all wars.

All this is no reason for drawing back from the struggle, but it is a good reason to be on our guard against being carried away by our own rhetoric – for the spirit of all crusades is a heady wine. We must, therefore, remain modest in our expectations, calmly analytical of past errors to avoid repeating them and, above all, conscious of the fact that whoever raises the weapon of revolution is wielding a two-edged sword, one edge of which is never far from his own heart.

PART FOUR

Blood Money?

Few things in recent times have done more to draw attention to the ethics of revolutionary violence than the grants made by the World Council of Churches to freedom organizations in Southern Africa. The arguments have raged in circles far wider than the official assemblies of the churches. Controversy is a great educator; the more people who are brought up sharply against these grave issues the better. But I feel much of the debate has been about what is really a secondary though not unimportant issue – whether or not the funds given to freedom movements have been used for humanitarian purposes as the donors intended. Of course, it matters a great deal that the leaders of the freedom movements should keep their promises, but the key to the issue is to be found elsewhere – in the age-old question whether Christians can themselves use force in the service of justice or actively encourage others to do the same. That question concerns me as a human being who hates violence, as an African leader whose people are in the front line of the freedom struggle and as a Christian anxious to do God's will. I have followed with great care the drift of the argument in Britain and throughout the West, and I confess myself baffled. I am not at all surprised that Christians are divided on the issue; it would be strange if it were otherwise. But I find the kind of arguments used

111

very odd and the quarters from which some of these arguments come even odder.

To judge from the outcry both from individual Christians and some official assemblies, one would have thought that throughout its long history the Christian Church has been a predominantly pacifist body and that the WCC in making these grants had broken with mainstream tradition. But is there really anything new in Christians supporting the use of force for what they believe to be moral ends? My encyclopaedia tells me that from the time of the Theban Legions in the second century AD, through the Crusades and right up to the present day when bishops bless nuclear submarines, the majority of Christians have supported the use of force under certain conditions. Christians have started some wars, served in many others and always prayed for a just victory – which they could surely not have done if they thought what they were doing was hateful to God?

I know that some splendid Christian people such as the Quakers refuse to have anything to do with war – I know this because some of them wrote to me once the freedom struggle in Rhodesia came to the boil, regretting my decision to back the freedom fighters. I am the black sheep of that flock now, I fear. Wonderful Christians as such folk are, they do not represent majority opinion in the Churches on this issue of peace and war – which does not necessarily mean they are wrong; minorities often get hold of an uncomfortable truth and will not let it go just because most of their fellows disagree with them.

But whatever else the WCC's action may have been, it was certainly orthodox. Why, then, were many Christians incensed by it? Could it have had something to do with the nature of the particular struggle in Southern Africa?

Another oddity is that amongst the most vociferous opponents of the WCC's action seem to be an extraordinarily high proportion of former military men, to judge from the correspondence columns of papers such as *The Daily Telegraph*. Retired generals, admirals and air force officers have been falling over one another to condemn the warlike activities of the WCC. I am curious to know what is the *muti* – magic medicine – in those grants which can turn men who fought in so many wars into such fervent pacifists. I can understand anyone who has seen the horrors of war at close range saying that he has come to the conclusion that it is futile to settle conflicts by force of arms, and he has resolved never to take up his sword again. But I do not think this is what many of these outraged military gentlemen are saying. I think most of them, having served their country well, would if the call came fight yet again. Nor, if everything they hold dear were threatened, would they, I think refuse whatever aid the churches could give them. Why, then, were they surprised and indignant that Zimbabwe freedom fighters did the same?

I came to know some of these British military men well when I took office as both President and Commander in Chief of Zambia's armed forces. I have always felt ill at ease in the various uniforms I must wear on military ceremonial occasions, and I suspect some of the senior British officers who were advising us at that time felt it a little sad that I had no medals to decorate my splendid uniforms. Possibly they thought I ought to award myself one or two! On the other hand I was intrigued by the rows and rows of brightly coloured ribbons they wore on their chests – red for blood, green for the jungle, yellow for the desert and so on. These men had fought in every part of the globe, and would be the first to admit they had helped turn a lot of it into smoking ruins. Why? If asked they would say something modest but I am sure they would talk about freedom and justice and democracy – all the things the freedom fighters in Southern Africa swear by too. These military men never doubted that God was on their side and that his Church should give them aid and comfort. But did not the enemy think the same? I saw that classic war film *All Quiet on the Western Front* at the Lusaka cinema. There is one scene I cannot forget – No Man's Land, with its mud, barbed wire and the bodies of German soldiers, and the motto carved on the belt buckle of each corpse was *Gott Mit Uns*. How could this be – God backing both sides? The Church backing both sides? Of course it is natural to believe that God is on our side in any conflict, but I would want to ask these military critics of the WCC: 'Which was *our* side in the Zimbabwe struggle?' I greatly fear that if they were to answer with absolute frankness, one might learn more about their racial attitudes than their theology.

That is a harsh judgement, can it be sustained? Well, take just one constant theme in these letters of protest from retired war heroes – the fact that white South Africans and Rhodesians fought alongside the British in two world wars. At the very least, so the argument runs, these old comrades must be supported in their time of need, and it is intolerable that the WCC should be giving comfort to their enemies. That is a powerful sentiment but hardly a noble one. I am embarrassed to have to point out that many more black than white Africans fought and died alongside the British in the last war – embarrassed because it is surely quite mad to determine one's loyalties according to the amount of blood spilt by one race rather than another in a war remote in time and circumstances from the matter at issue? But if we must take a racial census of the dead in military cemeteries, then on that pathetic reckoning there are ten times as many reasons for supporting blacks rather then whites in Southern Africa – though I am ashamed we should argue this way. Yet this is the logic of the 'wartime camaraderie' argument.

And if we must sink to this level of debate, it must be pointed out that the present South African government, which many of these military gentlemen are anxious to preserve, is formed from a Nationalist Party which has been fanatically anti-British throughout its history; indeed, some of its most prominent members were interned by Field Marshal Smuts during the Second World War for openly declaring their support for the Nazis. So just how much loyalty is owed to the Nationalists for their wartime performance? On the other hand, when Dr Milton Obote of Uganda was overthrown in a coup engineered by General Amin, there was widespread approval in Britain. One reason, openly stated, was that General Amin had been a British-trained NCO during the war and so would be a more reliable ally than Dr Obote. I have not heard that argument lately.

Enough of such dangerous nonsense! This line of argument is just plain racist and should be recognized as such. Retired soldiers and all who preach the 'kith and kin' doctrine in Britain will, no doubt, continue to stand behind their white ex-comrades of Southern Africa in the mistaken belief they are defending the last outposts of Christian civilization on the continent. And they will not see that this is a quite irrational basis on which to judge the Church in Africa generally or the WCC grants in particular. Most of us think with our blood when any issue is bedevilled by racial questions.

If I have gone on at length about these military critics of the WCC it is really to show how the heat generated by this issue melts the brains of the nicest people so that they end up denying to others the right to do the very thing of which they themselves are proudest – fight for freedom. I used to fear the military very much in the days when I was dodging the Federal Army, now I understand their mentality better because I have, let me say, professional dealings with them.

Soldiers have a deep, even exaggerated respect for authority and all the symbols of rank and uniform that go with it. I notice from war films (much of my education about the West comes from the cinema, which should be a terrible warning to someone!) that they salute even captured enemy officers of higher rank whom a few hours before they were trying to destroy. So there is a kind of freemasonry of the officer-class throughout the world which is, I suppose, a charming relic of the days of knightly chivalry. It only becomes dangerous when the officer-class must make judgements about conflicts of which they have little knowledge. Then by instinct they tend to support the killers in uniform rather than those in rags, and back governments against insurrectionists. This is because they have mostly gone to war on the orders of governments, and a lot of military activity this century has been concerned with putting down political insurrections. These attitudes also, I suspect, reflect the solidarity of the privileged. They back the status quo in most parts of the world because any change in the balance of power is, if not to their personal disadvantage, at least to the disadvantage of those with whom they naturally sympathize. And revolutions, like a rash, have a nasty habit of spreading!

All this I understand. I only become really angry when these Western critics of our struggle dismiss us as 'terrorists'. Whom do they call terrorists, these people who have bombed, blasted, burned and starved most of the earth at some time during this century? If we are of the same species at all, we are babes compared to those who planned and executed the blanket-bombing of Dresden, Warsaw and Coventry and many more cities, culminating in the ultimate horror of Hiroshima and Nagasaki. They have turned the seas to fire and poisoned the earth with chemical defoliants. They call *us* terrorists, these specialists in the use of the flame thrower, napalm and bacterial warfare?

Large-scale atrocities do not justify smaller ones, and we must judge the one as harshly as the other. But these old soldiers cannot call God as character-witness to the regrettable necessity of the terrible things they had to do in war and then scream with rage when the WCC through its actions implies that God might have a merciful word to say to us too about the terrible things we must do now.

It would be quite unnatural if people in Britain were not emotionally involved in the fate of their kith and kin in Zimbabwe and South Africa. We Africans have too strong a sense of family solidarity not to appreciate that. But someone has got to save these whites in Southern Africa from themselves. They have for a long time enjoyed a lifestyle which has made them the envy of the rest of the world – material prosperity in the sunny climes of some of the most beautiful countries on earth, plenty of land, cheap servants and salary levels most of those who were immigrants from Europe could never have achieved in their homelands. These whites have also had a superior status guaranteed by law, enshrined in custom and protected by force. This status bears no relationship to ability, personal qualities or contribution to national life but is determined solely by racial origins and skin pigmentation. This is what is now under threat, a theory and practice of racial superiority which will most assuredly be wiped off the face of the continent.

The writing has been on the wall for these people for a long time – a quite irresistible flood tide has been rolling southwards towards the tip of the continent since the end of the Second World War. Two hundred million Africans, having won freedom and human dignity for themselves, are determined that not a single one of their brothers and sisters will remain in chains. And the option is stark but not bleak. The whites can either give up willingly those privileges, based on their colour, which they ought never to have had, and then they can continue to enjoy a good life on terms of equality with their black fellow citizens, or they can cling a little longer to the privileges until things reach an explosive climax. And when the dust settles there will be no room for them on the continent on any terms.

No one who has got used to the Garden of Eden wants to leave it and adjust to a way of living whose quality depends on his hard work and courage. But this is what these whites must now do, and if their kith and kin in Britain encourage them to think otherwise they are helping to seal their doom.

Some of my critics will reply that the whites in Southern Africa have no other choice but to hang on to what they now possess because they will lose everything if and when the blacks take power. This fear is assiduously cultivated by

their leaders who have kept their jobs for so long by sup-
posingly demonstrating that they alone know how to
'handle' the blacks, which is the only policy issue that
really counts. Whites desperately seek reassurance that they
will not suffer the fate of their compatriots in states to the
north of them. What that 'fate' is they have no way of
knowing because powerful propaganda machines churn out
a ceaseless stream of horror stories about the hellish life in
countries like my own.

All right, we have had our troubles in Zambia, and it is
silly to imagine that it is possible to reverse the power-
relationship between the two races without a certain
amount of friction. We do not claim to be perfect; merely
human, and I would submit that any whites who are willing to be judged solely on their merits as human beings can
enjoy a good life in my country and others like it. We want
no exemption from being judged on the basis of the strict
truth – no whitewash, just the truth, seen both in the context of our colonial past and the perilous course we must
now set for mature nationhood. And this is surely where
these British kith and kin have a grave responsibility to
keep a sense of proportion and help their friends in Africa to
do the same.

Of course it is expecting a lot to ask white minorities
nurtured for generations on racist thinking to commit
themselves willingly into the hands of black majorities
who, so they have been falsely taught, are thousands of
years away from so-called civilized standards. But the
British people should know better; their education has not
been to the same extent utterly distorted by racist assumptions. Yet if they and their white kith and kin in Southern
Africa are going to feed each other's fear and hatred by

exchanging horror stories which go round and round as though in some closed system constantly recirculating poisonous waste, they will merely increase panic without offering any way out.

British sympathizers with the cause of the whites in Africa who encourage their kith and kin to continue their present policies, are like bystanders shouting to people trapped on the top floor of a burning building to stay put because rumour has it that the fire escape is unsafe. Such advice is an invitation to accept the certainty of extinction rather than take some degree of risk for a new lease of life. Right-wing politicians, the newspapers which are their mouthpieces and the whole 'kith and kin' lobby in Britain are cruelly raising false hopes in the minds of whites in Southern Africa if by making a great outcry on issues such as the WCC grants they give the impression they have the power to hurl back the forces of African liberation. It is one thing to share the anxiety of friends having to face up to hard realities; quite another to encourage them in the illusion that reality can be evaded. Whites must now make what John Foster Dulles once called an agonizing reappraisal of their position, and anything which inhibits them from coming to terms with what has always been unthinkable historically – life under black rule – must in the end make things impossible for them.

I suspect that many of the British critics of the WCC grants feel that outrage is expected of them as a gesture of loyalty to their beleaguered kith and kin in Africa. Silence might be taken for acquiescence in the shameful business of giving aid and comfort to the enemies of their friends. But the grants symbolize the precise opposite. They are saying that a responsible international body sees no reason to regard African freedom fighters as monsters intent on destroying the whites and all they stand for. The grants are not necessarily an uncritical endorsement of the freedom fighters' policies, but they *are* an uncritical endorsement of the freedom fighters' essential humanity. They are saying that these movements are not legions of Satan but children of God with a claim upon the compassion of the Christian Church. This ought to be cause for reassurance rather than foreboding on the part of whites wise enough to get at the complex truth underlying the easy but unhelpful distinctions between enemies and friends, them and us, blacks and whites – the terms in which the issue is usually expressed.

I fully accept that the WCC grants raise very difficult issues for the Churches; if they did not, the whole business would be trivial and hardly worth bothering about. Many of these hard questions are theological in nature and therefore beyond my competence. Let me state simply what the WCC's visionary action means to one African Christian who is both reassured and yet challenged by a prophetic deed which may well be seen in the future as decisive for the Church's fate in Southern Africa.

Off the Fence

I rejoice that the WCC grants are helping to combat the notion that the white minority government, in trying to exterminate the freedom fighters, is defending Christian civilization against a militant paganism that has spread across the rest of Africa. According to this fairy tale, Pretoria is a besieged fortress from which a holy war is being fought to uphold Christian values and standards. The South African regime in particular has always shown great ingenuity in finding scriptural authority to support its racial policies. Somewhere in the Bible there is bound to be a verse which can be twisted to justify anything this government does, however alien to the spirit of Christ. The Afrikaaner is a sad figure as he relives his past, seeing himself with a Bible in one hand and a gun in the other driving back the black hordes. Even if his account of history were true, which it is not, it would still not be a sound basis for action in the new Africa. But he is not of the new Africa, nor even of the old Africa, but of a private Africa, his own creation – just as his colour-conscious God and his segregated Kingdom of Heaven are his own creations.

It is a waste of time to confront these misguided defenders of the faith with statistics showing that black Africa, far from being a hotbed of paganism, is the fastest growing area of Christian influence in the world. Scholars say that by the end of this century a majority of the world's Christians will live in Africa. The white regimes will have none of it; their propaganda machines grind on, trying to convince world opinion that if they go under, so will Christianity. There is nothing new in this attempt to ident-ify Christianity and Western culture – to regard them as Siamese twins, joined in all their vital organs. Of course, it is impossible to import a Gospel without also importing the culture of the apostle who brings it. But it is utter nonsense to imply that the Gospel cannot survive the fall from political dominance of the culture in which it took shape at a particular period in history. Otherwise, in what way would it make sense to talk about Christianity as a world faith?

I know that the claim of the minority regime to be the last outpost of Christian civilization is utterly preposterous, though it is not for me to judge whether individuals within such a regime are Christian or not – only God can read their hearts. But certainly, they have no monopoly of Christian values and standards, and when their political tyranny is overthrown, that will not be a challenge to the Gospel but a vindication of it.

My greatest fear is that some of my African brothers and sisters may judge the Gospel by these people. They may think badly of Christianity because they assume the indignities of *apartheid* flow from the Gospel rather than out of defiance of it.

So the WCC grants are important in combating the smear that freedom fighters are seeking to destroy Christian civilization by toppling its supreme guardians on the African continent, the white minority regimes. Nor are we just talking about shot and counter-shot in a propaganda war. This is a world forum of Christianity utterly rejecting the terms in which the conflict in Africa is being portrayed as a battle between Christ and Anti-Christ. These are the Churches repudiating the false image of Christian civiliz-ation which the white regimes have raised up and wish to foist on the rest of the world. Hence, although the grants as gifts of money are important for their own sake as acts of practical compassion, the packaging, as it were, of theological argument in which these gifts come is equally important. This is what the minority regimes and their supporters really fear – not sums of money hardly big enough to make much difference to the outcome of the struggle, but the big truths which stand behind the money. They *could* affect the outcome of the struggle.

Of course we must not go to the opposite extreme and make the mistake of standing the crazy theology of Afrikaanerdom on its head and regard these grants as proof that God is on the side of the freedom fighters and it is our enemies who are Anti-Christ. I must confess that according to my reading of the Gospel, Jesus proclaimed a God who seems to have a pronounced bias in favour of the poor, the outcast and the oppressed, who puts princes to rout and raises the humble high. It is hard to imagine such a God frowning upon the crusade of Africa's people for freedom and justice. But we must not presume on God's favour; we can only seek to deserve it. All of us, black and white, oppressed and oppressors, are miserable sinners standing under judgement. So if I rejoice at the WCC's action, it is not because I wish to enlist that body's support in turning the freedom struggle into a holy war. Quite the contrary. The war in Southern Africa is neither more nor less holy than any other war. It is a messy, brutal, degrading business, and if we forget that and come to enjoy the killing game, we shall end up gaining political rights but losing our essential humanity.

Because this struggle, like all wars, *is* such a dreadful enterprise, the support of the WCC is all the more precious because it is a rare example of the Churches being prepared to abandon the role of moral referee at a safe distance and take the risk of being compromised by controversial action. To be fair, the Churches in the West have passed many resolutions condemning the white minority regimes and expressing support for the oppressed people of Southern Africa, but this support is usually carefully hedged about by all sorts of qualifications and sermonizing about the self-defeating nature of violence. I have no wish to be unkind, but what these resolutions boil down to (and I have files full of them) is one simple proposition – *apartheid* is evil and must be overthrown and the oppressed people have the support of the Churches provided they do not do the one thing necessary to overthrow it.

Such advice is well-meant, but it is unhelpful, even a little hypocritical. Any Church which is on record as having declared that it would not support the use of force in defence of Britain's freedom can speak with some authority. But it is really no use Churches which refuse to make pacifism their official policy telling us that pacifism is the only Christian way. To affirm the moral and even theological necessity for radical change but at the same time outlaw the only way of getting it, is to cast a vote in favour of an oppressive status quo. If additionally, these Western Churches have a financial stake possibly by historical accident rather than choice in the survival of an international economic system of which regimes like that of South Africa are cornerstones, then their lofty moral arbitration seems a little suspect. To damn a system and then urge those fighting it to use only methods which will do it no great harm hardly gives the impression that the Churches really mean business.

Certainly, the WCC, in coming off the fence on the Southern Africa issue, has run the risk of being seriously misunderstood. The trouble with those who actually do something about their moral choices is that they could, in the event, be proved wrong; it is much safer to state ultimate principles and then allow the interested parties to apply them to the specific issue. That way the Church's objectivity can be safeguarded so that it remains uncompromised – but not very serviceable.

I do not understand the Bible to be saying anything like this about God's way of saving us. He did not remain in heaven, looking down sadly upon the world whilst things got worse and worse, sending down messages of good advice through his servants, the prophets. Surely the whole point about the Incarnation is that God in the person of Jesus actually came down from heaven and got embroiled in the whole mess. And the moment he stepped into history, he took the risk of bringing Divinity into disrepute, he laid himself open to misunderstanding, he did and said things which were not only damaging to his moral reputation but also to any claim to infallibility. When he offered himself to be baptised by John in the River Jordan, he stepped into water which had been dirtied by thousands of sinners. That is how he saw his mission, as sharing the same life, breathing the same air, accepting the same limitations as his fellow human beings. That is how I see him in my mind's eye when I recite those words in the creed, 'He came down from heaven, and became man . . .'.

I see the Church which remains safely remote from the conflict, making statements of principle, as non-incarnational (if there is such a word), and I see the WCC's action as an example of truly incarnational theology in practice; like Jesus in the River Jordan, it is being baptised into the conflict and running the risk of getting dirty. Of course, it might be charged that I take this lofty view of the WCC's action because it has weighed in on our side of the issue and I might not be so enthusiastic if it had decided to give grants to the South African Government instead. That is a fair point, but I feel so deeply about the whole matter that I would go so far as to accept that any Church which gave practical support to the white regimes in Southern

Africa was at least backing its moral principles with costly action. And provided there is respectable biblical support for what it does, then I have no complaint.

I suppose I can afford to be so magnanimous because I have great faith in the Church's wisdom. In the end she will be faithful to her Lord and the truth of Scripture, so I am prepared to take the risk of preaching so firmly the virtues of an incarnational witness, even though there is a remote possibility the Church might settle for the other side!

What arrogance it is for us human beings to drag God and his Church into our squabbles and try to win them for our side. The issue is not whether God is on our side, but whether we are on God's side. On this I am no authority and would humbly seek the Church's guidance, hoping always that this guidance will take a practical form like the WCC grants rather than elegant resolutions!

The WCC grants are bound to spark off renewed discussion within the Churches about the nature of violence, and the way in which the terms of the debate are defined will be an important test both of the honesty of Christians and of their courage in facing painful truths. Someone has said that history is written by the victor. By the same token, violence has always been defined by the powerful rather than the weak, the oppressor rather than the oppressed. The mighty of the earth have at their disposal not only armies and police forces but control of the media and the shaping of the educational system. So they are able to define violence as any concerted action by the oppressed which threatens their monopoly of power.

The Churches, not only as a matter of elementary justice but also because the God they worship is biased in favour of the oppressed, must see the world through his eyes, share the humiliation of the poor and give the dumb a voice. They must re-write the dictionary, these good Churchmen, and define violence by studying the everyday experience of the oppressed. To starve people is violence, to segregate them into ghettos, treat them as second-class citizens, deny them political rights and economic opportunities – all these things are violence. What nonsense is the claim by the white-dominated establishments of Southern Africa and their supporters that the black terrorist is disrupting a peaceful society and introducing violence where none existed before he came on the scene. The freedom fighter is not importing violence into a happy nation; he is responding pathetically, desperately, to the vastly greater institutional violence which hides behind the majesty of the law in white minority regimes.

It is virtually impossible to be non-violent in an unjust society. If we are not acting to change things – which must evoke violence from those who will do anything to protect privilege – we are, in our passivity, throwing our weight on the side of the oppressor. Even the preaching of passive resistance in an unjust society will have consequences the preacher could not have foreseen and which he might wish to repudiate. I yield to no one in my love and admiration for Martin Luther King, but it must be obvious to anyone who understands both the pride and despair of American blacks that Dr King in holding up before the downtrodden the vision of a land of the free and a home of the brave, was liberating powerful forces in the black soul. As he shared with his people in great preaching his dream of an America in which people would be judged by the content of their character rather than the colour of their skins, he was lighting a powder keg. Of course he preached always the power of the Cross and the supremacy of love as a revolutionary force, and it would be an insult to his memory to suggest that his words could have had more than one meaning. But in all realism, those words could have more than one effect on particular hearers. Once you encourage a slave to think and act like a man, it is like awakening a Gulliver pinned to the ground with threads by Lilliputians – even in the act of standing erect he tears apart the system within which he has been imprisoned.

I can speak with some authority about this, for I too have addressed vast crowds and been not only very moved but more than a little frightened by the response of the people. It has to do with this question of definitions – the meaning of words is determined not simply by the intention of the speaker but also by the experience of the hearers. We discovered this truth during the unhappy years before we attained independence. Such terms as 'partnership' and 'Federation' had one meaning for whites and quite a different one for us – *they* were talking about a political device whose purpose was to make provision for the infinitely slow advancement of the African people in ways which would not jeopardize white supremacy – *we* were talking about an evil system which institutionalized racism and denied our legitimate political aspirations. Same words, different meanings.

So it is with this debate about violence. Whose definition are we going to use – that of the oppressed or of the oppressor? So far as I can judge from the British press, the white-dominated regimes of Southern Africa have been allowed to dictate the terms of the debate. They say violence is anything which threatens the structures of power; they do not define as violence the means they use to exert their mastery. Certainly, the Western Churches have questioned the ethics of these power structures. I must admit, however, to some disappointment at the tendency of some Church leaders to speak both in the language of the oppressed and of the oppressor. It is possible to be too reasonable, too accommodating, too much able to see the viewpoint of both sides in a dispute, and too anxious to keep on good terms with everyone. In some situations this attitude would be quite admirable but it is a moral luxury permitted only to those far remote geographically and mentally from the revolution. So far as we in Africa are concerned, there can be no neutrality. And the WCC in making these grants to our freedom fighters and robustly defending what it has done, has come down off the fence, and by that one action has secured for the Church, or at least that part of it which stands behind the WCC, a respectful hearing in the new Africa. For it has shown it knows how to speak in the vernacular of the victim, and that is not a language one can learn from the textbooks.

It is difficult to exaggerate the importance of the debate stimulated within the Churches by the WCC grants; what is not so widely realized is that these grants have also created heated discussion in the freedom movements also. If some sincere churchmen doubt the wisdom of making the grants, some sincere freedom fighters doubt the wisdom of accepting them. Throughout her history, Africa has been the recipient of many gifts from the West, not all of which have been unmixed blessings. It is fashionable in certain quarters to slander the leaders of the freedom movements as ideological harlots, prepared to sell their loyalty to whoever offers the highest price. There is an element of sheer political illiteracy about such sneers, of course, since their complete rebuttal rests in the simple fact that the freedom struggle is not yet over in Southern Africa. Efficient though the war machine of South Africa may be, there are powers in the world so irresistible that they would have settled the issue by now had they been invited to take a hand. But the freedom movements have no intention of piling up debts and obligations which may have to be repaid with interest once victory has been won. So all offers of help are received with appreciation but not all are accepted. We would rather fight with our bare hands than touch the gleaming machinery proffered from some dubious quarters.

If the offer of these grants says something important about the Churches, the acceptance of them says something equally important about the freedom movements. They mark a new era in relationships – in some senses a reversal of a century or more of the particular dealings between the Christian Churches and the African people which were unwholesome and demeaning. The very nature of the grants and the spirit in which they have been given rules out any suggestion that this is the Church yet again trying to shape Africa's future for her. Even more than this, I hear the WCC acknowledging that the freedom struggle is also about the liberation of the oppressor, releasing him from evil racist and totalitarian notions which if allowed to remain unchecked must mean the death of his soul. We are not just fighting for African freedom but for the health of the whole human race, for poison present in any part of the organism pollutes the whole body.

I have deliberately avoided dwelling at any length on the fact that the WCC grants have been given and accepted for strictly humanitarian purposes, though I am in a position to confirm that the conditions have been honoured – the Church's money has bought medicine and clothes and shelter rather than guns and other implements of war. If I seem to have brushed this aspect aside, it is not because I think it unimportant – how could I, when my own family received similar help from Christians in Northern Rhodesia when I was on the run from the security forces a long time ago? But I think there is no profit in pursuing arguments about whether or not any money given for humanitárian purposes will free an equivalent amount to buy armaments. This is to dabble in the economics of fairy land rather than the real, confused world of war. I know, for instance, that the Red Cross has poured many hundreds of thousands of pounds into Southern Africa in aid, and so have other relief agencies concerned with the plight of refugees and other victims of the struggle. Can those who wish to oppose the WCC grant on these grounds claim to be able to track down every penny of Red Cross relief money to the recipients *and beyond*? Can they show, given the interlocking nature of all economic relationships, that the result of feeding some refugees was not to relieve the Smith Government of one bit of that burden, so freeing more money for the Rhodesian war machine? And would they stop supporting that admirable organization, the Red Cross, as a result? Such arguments are utterly sterile and really mask the true motives of those who do not wish, for quite different reasons, to see justice done in Southern Africa.

What sort of creatures do these critics of the WCC grants think we Africans are? Do they imagine we enjoy seeing our children go without adequate food, our old people denied a sheltered place in which to rest their heads, our wives suffering without proper medical care? Are we so crazy with blood lust, we terrorists, that we will turn deaf ears to the agony of our nearest and dearest in our eagerness to buy guns rather than bread? I will ask those who accuse us of misusing the WCC grants this one simple question – if their children were sick and in need of medicines and the WCC offered money to buy drugs, would they, in their right minds, go to the armament market for hand grenades instead? Of course they would not! Do they then think we love our children less than they love theirs?

I am trying to put into words the terrible truth that those who are forced to fight for freedom against great odds and with strictly limited resources have to make choices which tear them apart – between the need to have something to fight with and the claims of their families. And most of these families willingly accept sacrifices in the cause of freedom – as did the people on the home front in Britain during the Second World War. The guerrillas will find the means to fight anyway, that is the nature of the urge to be free, but if the suffering of their families is eased by humanitarian agencies such as the WCC, then they will be truly grateful and see that the intentions of the donors are honoured. And the Churches will only be doing what they have done throughout Christian history – helping the victims of war without regard to issues of grand strategy such as: whose side will be helped to victory by our practical compassion?

Following Jesus

I have before me a letter in which a white brother, obviously a Christian and a civilized man, takes me to task for supporting the freedom struggle. He is sad about my attitudes and feels that I have fallen from grace. He beseeches me to imagine Jesus as he was in the days of his flesh walking through the Central African bush instead of the Palestinian desert. Now, he asks, can you see Jesus murdering missionaries, planting landmines, intimidating African villagers, or giving his blessing to those who do? Well, no, I cannot truthfully see Jesus doing any of these things, nor can I imagine him giving his blessing to the organized violence of the white minority regimes either. I cannot see him standing by passively whilst one race brutalizes another, using the army and police to do it, all the time claiming it is being done for his sake – to protect *Christian* civilization. So I do not think this kind of argument gets us much further. We all want to drag Jesus in on our side in these differences of opinion, borrow his authority and twist his words to support our case. In fact, I am sure we are so far adrift from truly understanding what he really meant that he must weep for us all.

My white friend ends his letter by exhorting me to turn from my wicked ways and follow Jesus who, he claims, rejected violence in favour of love and chose to be a spiritual rather than political leader. How simple my friend makes it all seem! He *knows* what Jesus would do if he were in my shoes or in the shoes of the leaders of the Patriotic Front. How can some Christians be so sure they are able to read Jesus's mind? Apparently by choosing those bits of his teaching which fit their case and disregarding those which do not, or getting academic in order to prove that some parts of the Gospel are genuine whilst others were written later or by someone else. And by good fortune the genuine passages happen to support their position. Truly, if a politician tried to get away with half the things some Christian scholars do, he would be pelted with mealies at every public meeting – not just for being slippery but for being so obvious about it!

It is strange that when we Christians want to recruit Jesus to our cause we seem to have little difficulty in showing that whatever may be uncertain in the Gospels, one thing is plain – Jesus was one of *us*; whatever we are against, so was he – drink, divorce, violence, politics. Those parts of his teaching which say so are undoubtedly genuine, no matter how much doubt is cast on other parts. The more we Christians play this game, the more convinced I am that my father, David Julizya Kaunda, was on safer ground in believing every single word of the Bible. Such a belief is dismissed as crude these days, and in many ways it was, but I do not think it is half so dangerous a pastime as picking and choosing texts that suit our opinions. If my father's way was too hard, then that way is too easy.

I respect those Christians who reject killing under any circumstances because the Gospel forbids it, provided they give the same absolute authority to everything else Jesus said. Yet even then I have my problems. This is Easter time and I have been listening to a service of worship on Zambia Radio. The theme was the *living* Christ; the hymns, lessons, prayers and sermon all drumming home the point that the life of Jesus did not come to an end on Calvary – he goes marching on today and every day until the end of the world. I say 'Amen!' to that. And I want to say this also. If we take the Easter story seriously, the question we should be asking is not only, 'What did Jesus do in Palestine long ago?' but 'What is he doing *today*?' In other words, the latest news we have of his acts and attitudes is not contained in the Gospels but in our daily newspaper. He is at work at the heart of the tension in Southern Africa. But how and where? Well, I think we must take what he did in first-century Palestine as a series of pointers to what he is doing amongst us – and that is what God has always been doing since Moses led the Israelites out of Egypt – freeing men and women from every form of slavery, political as well as spiritual.

We know what God's goal is, but I do not believe that isolated sentences from the Gospels can be used as a complete plan of campaign for achieving that goal. Nor, on the other hand, would I dare to suggest that we can completely ignore his words from the Gospels and just assume that he is on our side whatever we do. We agonize in seeking his will, knowing we may be terribly wrong, but getting confidence from the whole message of the Bible. That message, in a sentence, says God is bringing to birth a new age in which the oppressed will be free, the downtrodden will be lifted up and there will be fresh life for all. There's a Negro spiritual I love to sing, and one verse runs:

> Slavery chain done broke at last, broke at last,
> broke at last
> Slavery chain done broke at last,
> Going to praise God till I die . . .

That is what the Gospel is about. For this reason, politics and religion move in step like twin horses harnessed together, pulling God's chariot. And though I would not be so foolish as to argue that God ordains violence in the battle against all forms of oppression, I have hope that those who are driven to extremes in order to break slavery's chain will receive his mercy.

Some of my Christian friends tell me that to be a disciple of Jesus I must obey with absolute literalism his commandment against killing. I am certainly tied up in knots by that commandment, but I do wonder whether Christian pacifists take quite so seriously as they ought some of Jesus's other instructions. What about his insistence that we should not resist evil *at all*, by fair means or foul, peaceful methods or force? How does my white correspondent who attacks me for disobeying one of Jesus's commandments explain the fact that in advocating passive resistance he is proposing that we break another commandment? I do hope he will not reply by playing that game of picking and choosing texts again.

I would ask my friend whether he would seriously expect me as a Head of State not to resist evil – disband the police force, send the army home, empty the prisons and hope for the best? If not, where is the logic in being absolute about one commandment but allowing exceptions from another? He, no doubt, would point out that there are different shades of pacifist conviction, some more absolute than others. Just so – even as there are different shades of non-pacifist conviction, and if I do not condemn him for being unable to live a life of Christian perfection on earth, so I would expect some recognition that those of us on the other side of the line are not all anti-Christian monsters. We all live by faith, under Judgement, but relying on God's mercy when we fall short of the standards Christ set us.

Dear Lord! How does one run a country by sticking to the letter of Jesus's teaching? He not only rules out guerrilla warfare but also those tactics of passive resistance which have been proposed as humane alternatives to armed struggle in Southern Africa. He will not choose between one weapon and another by implying that the policeman's truncheon is preferable to the terrorist's bayonet, nor does he want the state involved in disputes at all. He neither approves of civil disobedience nor of the civil authorities who are being disobeyed. When I led UNIP's freedom struggle and insisted on the method's of positive non-violence, I thought that such a strategy would be acceptable to Christ in a way that armed struggle was not. But Jesus seems to brush all these distinctions aside. It may be a matter of common sense or plain morality that no one in his right mind would advocate and use violence if there were some way of securing justice peacefully. But Jesus does not appear to be concerned even with common sense. As I read the Sermon on the Mount, if we practise any form of resistance to evil, we have strayed from Christ's teaching, and both pacifist and non-pacifist alike stand condemned.

Hence, if we Christians who are concerned to achieve justice in Southern Africa are barred by the words of Jesus from using either armed struggle or passive resistance, what is left to us? Either to stand back from the battle and allow those who are not bound by the words of Jesus to do our fighting for us; or else we can pray and hope that in God's good time, oppressive regimes may see the error of their ways and grant justice and human rights freely to their victims even at the expense of their own privileged status. This is not the way it has been throughout history. Who can doubt that but for the freedom fighters' efforts, Mr Ian Smith and his successors would be thumbing their noses to world opinion ten years from now?

If Christ outlaws all resistance to injustice, armed or peaceful, then what is going to change things? Do we wait until he returns in glory, grimly accepting that there can be no justice until then? Or are we Christians condemned to be perpetual spectators, wagging our fingers in regret as non-Christians march into battle, but still claiming our place in the sun when the shooting stops? For all the peoples of Southern Africa will be free whether or not we are in the ranks of the liberators. Are nationalists, Marxists, humanitarians and liberal democrats all to do their bit to smash oppressive regimes whilst Christians lament their inability to join in the struggle but still expect the liberated peoples to give a ready ear to the Gospel? Why should they? The Church may indeed have been where the battle was hottest helping the stricken to die like Christians, but once the people are free they will listen with the greatest respect to those who helped them to live like human beings.

I can see that a cadre of Christians of heroic stature who went where the fight was fiercest and accepted freely the way of the Cross, offering no resistance when they were led like sheep to the slaughter, would be making a powerful witness to the Gospel. And who can tell how God might use their self-sacrifice? Their blood might truly be the seed of the Church in the new Africa. And there would be a glorious certainty about their actions – they need not waste time watering down Christ's harsh demands by twisting texts this way and that. They would accept his demands at face value without argument. But I must ask, a little shamefacedly, is this the only way for one who seeks to follow Christ? If so I do not see how it is possible both to be a Christian and practise my profession, politics, which involves trafficking in forms of power which cannot be reconciled with the ethics of the Cross. I do not see how a

Head of State can be a pacifist, let alone organize government on the principle of not resisting evil. Ordered life
would be impossible.

The Christian perfectionist will retort that there is a
higher law than that of good order which comes into play
in spite of (or possibly because of) the resulting chaos – the
law of the Kingdom of Heaven. Indeed so, but as a leader
who has sworn a solemn oath to protect and defend all the
people of Zambia, how can I *compel* my fellow countrymen
to act according to the law of love unto death without
making nonsense of the Gospel? Many of our citizens are
devout Jews, Hindus, Muslims or follow traditional
African religions which do not preach the gospel of non-
resistance to evil.

This is surely the heart of the Christian leader's dilemma.
He is under orders from our Lord to live according to some
very tough laws – and this he may be able to do personally
if he has enough faith. But by what right does he enjoin
those laws on people who do not share his faith? One
possible answer might be that these 'laws' of Christ are not
laws in the political or constitutional sense at all; they are
dispositions of the heart. Yet if these laws do not spill over
and become the raw material of political programmes, then
people like me end up practising a Christianity which is
personal and private, and try to run our public lives according to less demanding rules which can be obeyed by Christians and non-Christians alike. If I really believed that, then
the whole of my adult life would have been wasted on an
impossible dream – a Kingdom whose boundaries enclose
the whole of life and whose revolutionary power will
transform man's politics, economics and social life as well as
his inner nature.

I fear that on this issue of violence, Christ is putting a pistol to my head, or rather, pointing a Cross at my heart. As a political leader I cannot accept that Cross as the standard for my public life; as a penitent sinner I cannot evade it. I know of no way out of that awful predicament.

PART FIVE

'War is Hell!'

We have been talking about violence as though it were a single terrible thing. But of course there are all kinds and degrees of violence and if we fail to recognize this we shall end up admitting sadly that violence is beyond or beneath moral judgement – once the shooting starts civilized behaviour is no longer possible and the rulebook flies out of the window. We must be on our guard against thinking of war as a vast natural force like a flood or famine or earthquake, otherwise it will seem as futile to apportion responsibility for the conflict in Zimbabwe for instance as to pin the blame on someone for a tornado.

It is customary to talk about a war 'breaking out' as though it were a bush fire in which a tuft of grass begins to smoulder and soon there are flames everywhere without any human agency being to blame. But wars do not 'break out' in this sense; someone causes them although it may sometimes be hard to identify the original aggressor. Equally when I read of a nation 'drifting into' war I do not know what is meant – this is another of those phrases which mislead us into thinking that wars are not human creations but scourges like the plague sent by the gods. On this reckoning violence has no human agents, only human victims.

It was General William Tecumseh Sherman who, during the American Civil War, coined the phrase, 'War is Hell!' According to Professor Michael Walzer of Harvard University, to whom I am indebted for some of the argument which follows, by these words General Sherman meant two things; one was a description, the other a moral defence. Firstly, war creates a condition quite outside ordinary human experience, in which brutality and destruction on a vast scale cause untold suffering to such an extent that those who bear the full brunt of it may be said to be in hell. But secondly, General Sherman was suggesting that once a war has started, all normal rules of human conduct are suspended and whatever terrible things men do in battle may be excused just so long as theirs was not the side which fired the first shot.

This is a very dangerous doctrine. It implies that an aggressor has lost all human rights – whatever horrible things must be done to defeat him are permissible because he started the whole business. So President Truman could argue that he was right to drop atom bombs on Hiroshima and Nagasaki because the Japanese had started the war, and everything else, including nuclear destruction, followed from this fact.

On a much smaller scale, this same doctrine was at work in the Zimbabwe freedom struggle when security forces punished a whole village because there had been some guerrilla activity in the area. The practice of levying collective fines on poor people, closing down their schools and clinics, sometimes even burning down their huts and slaughtering their cattle – all these things were daily happenings in that war. And they, together with other acts much worse, were justified by an appeal to General Sherman's philosophy. Just as the raid on Pearl Harbour in 1941 excused the nuclear

destruction of two Japanese cities in 1945, so a shot from
the vicinity of a Zimbabwean village led to its extinction.
Of course these two examples are not to be compared in
scale, but I insist the morality is the same. Just as the
morality was the same when guerrillas committed atrocities
upon innocent villagers because someone had betrayed their
comrades to the police. War *is* hell alright, but it is a different hell from the one the Bible describes; there, only
those who deserve punishment actually suffer, whereas in
the inferno of war it is usually the innocent who bear the
brunt of pain.

What I am trying to get at is some moral distinction between the reason why a war is fought and the way in which
it is fought. I know why the Zimbabwean guerrillas and
the security forces were killing each other and a lot of innocent people as well, and I think I know who will be judged
in the end to have brought about this tragedy. Yet the
question: who is to blame? is surely not the only one we
must answer if we are to hang on to some bits and pieces of
civilized behaviour. Even within the hell of war there are
individual acts of mercy or brutality done, and we must not
give up the attempt to apply moral judgements to them
otherwise we shall be accepting a debased view of man. We
shall be saying, in effect, that war really shows up man for
what he is; it strips the layers of civilization off him and he
charges away like an angry elephant, flattening everything
in sight. Possibly that is how it looks (or feels if we happen
to be in the elephant's path), but this same beast did not
tread on that little clump of African violets and avoided
knocking down that poor man's hut and did not tear those
young calves to pieces. And we should notice these things
and set them against the general trail of destruction.

We get our hope from some strange places. I have a collection of pamphlets the ex-Rhodesia Government used to distribute throughout the Tribal Trust Lands during periodic security sweeps. They show pictures of the mutilated bodies of dead Africans who are supposedly identified as 'terrorists' and the text contains crude descriptions of the punishment which would be meted out to village people who did not betray to the army any guerrillas in the area. They are not very clever weapons of propaganda because those who compiled them have no real understanding of the people to whom they are addressed. But the interesting thing to me is that every single pamphlet has at least one paragraph which is a sort of small sermon justifying the Government's actions. Now why bother to make such excuses? A soldier might say that it is tactically important for a government fighting a guerrilla war to win the hearts and minds of the ordinary people. I think the true explanation lies deeper.

Throughout history, tyrants guilty of terrible crimes against humanity have been very concerned to prove that they were in the right. Even when it seemed they had conquered the world, they still destroyed evidence of their atrocities and tried to rewrite history. Why? Who was left of sufficient importance that his disapproval might worry such a dictator?

My love for war films furnishes another example. I recall accounts of the experiences of Allied soldiers who were POWs in German hands during the Second World War. Conditions in some of the camps were, by all accounts, very bad. But when the time drew near for a visit from the representatives of the International Red Cross, a certain amount of window dressing was done in the camps to make the prisoners' lives seem much pleasanter than they really were. Now why should a nation at war with half the world care about the reactions of a handful of visiting humanitarians based in a tiny country like Switzerland? The answer cannot simply be that Hitler wished to keep world opinion on his side. Very few nations, none of them powerful, were neutral; the rest were either fighting for him or against him and so their opinions were already formed. I prefer to believe that even in the middle of a war which is violating all the rules of civilized behaviour, both sides still have this need to convince *someone* that their cause is just and it is their enemies who are perpetrating crimes against humanity.

Who, then, is this *someone* whose opinion of our actions in war matters enough for us to organize propaganda campaigns to show that right is on our side? And we all do it. Take the question of the assassination of Archbishop Luwum by Amin. Why did that madman go to all the trouble of trying to convince the world that the Archbishop had been killed in a car crash? Why did he not just boast openly that he had destroyed the Archbishop in the same way and for the same reason that he had rid himself of thousands of less prominent opponents of his regime – because they refused to treat him like some crazy god?

To take another case – the murder of some missionaries in Zimbabwe. The security forces blamed the guerrillas; the guerrillas insisted that missionaries were amongst the few influential friends they possessed in Zimbabwe and so the Selous Scouts must have done the killings in order to outrage the Church and serve as a warning to other missionaries. The struggle for freedom in Zimbabwe developed into a filthy war before the end, so in all the ocean of blood-letting what did the few drops of blood shed by a handful of missionaries or by innocent villagers really count? And why did both sides go to such lengths to plead their own innocence and point the finger at someone else?

It seems as though within the massive immorality of war there is still a mini-morality at work. When you think of the tidal wave of destruction that both sides unleashed in the Second World War by air, sea and land, is it not significant that fliers who had used devilish devices to destroy thousands of human lives on the ground would still be indignant if they were accused of shooting at an enemy airman parachuting down from his crashing aircraft? And what about generals on whose orders artillery reduced whole cities to rubble, who would still courtmartial any of their soldiers seen killing enemy troops trying to surrender or caught bayoneting wounded opponents? War, as General Sherman claimed, may be hell, but there are apparently still codes of conduct to be observed in the middle of the inferno. This is a very curious thing. On the one hand we outlaw wars of aggression and yet lay down laws such as the Geneva Convention which spell out how these wars should be fought.

I ask again, who is this *someone* whose disapproval even the Hitlers of this world will seek to deflect by hiding evidence of some atrocities whilst openly glorying in atrocities of much greater magnitude? I believe this *someone* to be none other than you and me, not because of our rank or profession or influence but simply as moral beings – bearers of a universal notion of right and wrong that will just not go away no matter how hard we try to wipe it off the face of the earth. To appeal to something called 'the judgement of history' seems hardly worthwhile because aggressors do not worry too much how they will be described in the history books. And if there is such an organ as 'the moral conscience of mankind' it takes so long to make itself felt as to have very little deterrent effect. And yet it is along these lines that we must seek for some explanation of the strange anxiety of those who engage in violence to try to show they are right. At the end of the day, the judgement of history is not delivered by lawyers and scholars nor is it derived from some body of case law. It is a general agreement amongst people like you and me which does not come about because we have put our heads together in some universal convention but rises within us like the grief or happiness which can grip a whole community.

I know this is a vague, unsatisfactory, some might even say, sentimental, view of human affairs, but I happen to believe that our dealings with each other are governed by a moral law which though almost universally broken is still recognizable. There are, I believe, some sentiments so much a part of our moral nature, some truths so evident that it is impossible to analyse them and almost a waste of time discussing them, yet they are *there*, and when we suppress them we do violence to our basic nature. This is a fundamental humanist conviction.

The notion of what is right and wrong goes right back to the earliest records of human conflict. The Old Testament sets out in a number of passages rules for the conduct of war, and Professor Walzer quotes a charming and civilized paragraph from an early Indian manual of international law which lays it down that the following kinds of people must not be dragged into the business of killing and being killed, 'Those who look on without taking part, those afflicted with grief. . . . those who are asleep, thirsty or fatigued or are walking along the road, or have a task in hand unfinished, or who are proficient in fine art'.

We have refined the categories of noncombatants since then and tend, I am afraid, to describe them in the cold terminology of the lawyer rather than the language of the poet, but the principle still holds good, and always has done – that some limits must be placed upon the use of violence. This conviction has survived mankind's triumphal progress from the wars of chivalry to blanket-bombing. The principle may be vague and frail but like a tiny thread it runs through human history.

Were not the Nuremberg Trials at the end of the Second World War only justifiable as a rather cumbersome way of stating humanity's sense of moral outrage at what the accused had done? We might worry about whether the right people were in the dock or whether some of us, their accusers, ought not to have been in the dock with them. We may have doubts about the realism of trying to turn the making of war into a crime punishable in a court of law and question how legal responsibility can be divided out amongst political leaders, generals and those who obeyed their orders. We may wonder many things about these unique happenings in the city of Nuremberg, but my own conclusion is that the trials were justified, and only justified, as an affirmation by mankind that this is still a moral world. It will only remain so just as long as we can still get some consensus, however crude and unsatisfactory, about what forms of behaviour cannot be tolerated if the term 'humanity' is to have any meaning when used to describe our species.

I am an old-fashioned moralist who believes that there

are certain laws written in all men's hearts rather than on
the statute books, and when in the heat of conflict men
violate these laws they know what they have done. God
help us, there may be times when under the stress of extreme necessity we have no option but to deny the noblest
part of our nature, but let us not take refuge from the full
acceptance of moral responsibility behind a smokescreen of
propaganda or a rewriting of history or some appeal to a
'War is hell!' philosophy. We must insist that wars are not
acts of God nor are they fought by robots or dehumanized
creatures, but by breathing, thinking and feeling men and
women who know right from wrong.

I need no one to point out that such a simple belief,
however passionately held, can hardly survive the battering
our system takes when all the ethical dilemmas of modern
war are hurled against it. But if we are driven to acts which
of their nature call out deep feelings of guilt and shame
from us, then our uneasy consciences must serve to remind
us that when all is said and done we are still moral beings
who can only engage in war at the price of setting up
terrible tensions within us.

There are certain places whose names mark off particularly black spots from the surrounding greyness of general
war – Guernica in Spain, Lidice in Poland, My Lai in Vietnam – and nearer home, Karima and St Faith's Mission in
Zimbabwe, Williamo in Mozambique. In these places and
others like them deeds were done which stand out from the
confusion and generalized brutality of war as crimes against
humanity by the most rough and ready standards of justice.
It is a terrible thing to say, but these are names which
ought to stir up hope in our hearts whenever we hear them,
because they remind us that even in the hell of war, just

occasionally mankind said, 'No! Enough is enough!'.

It is not too hard to spot a crime in peaceful times, but so long as we are still able to do the same at the heart of great conflicts then I will resolutely stick to my belief that we live in a moral world – and know it.

Guerrillas or Terrorists?

On 27 June 1976, the Speaker of the rebel Rhodesian parliament ruled that he would no longer allow members to use the terms 'guerrilla' and 'freedom fighter' during the course of debates in the House. The correct name, he said, was 'terrorist'. There is more at stake here than a question of labels, though our use of highly emotive terms can sometimes betray our deeper feelings. When Joshua Nkomo's house in Lusaka was attacked and destroyed by Rhodesian forces in April 1979, the British press referred to the invaders as a column of Rhodesian 'commandos' – which is, I believe, a highly honorific term because of its association with the famous British fighting force. And yet that same press invariably described units of the Patriotic Front, loyal Zimbabweans fighting in and for their own country, as 'terrorists'.

It is really not worthwhile getting drawn into the game of smear and counter-smear. My concern is to keep alive some vestige of decency in the freedom struggle, and if we are to make accurate moral judgements then we must use the terms 'guerrillas' and 'terrorists' as they are understood not by the propaganda merchants but by the international conventions. These are quite distinct forms of violence which fall into different moral categories, so we must unswervingly make the effort to use 'guerrilla' and 'terrorist' as words of description rather than terms of abuse.

As I understand it, the essence of guerrilla warfare is the use of small, mobile forces who operate in the midst of a generally sympathetic civilian population and whose basic weapon is surprise. They achieve surprise partly because of their mobility and partly because the guerrilla fighter is hard to distinguish from the rest of the people. This is, of course, one of his great strengths and the security force's greatest problem – they find themselves having to make war on the people in order to 'get at' the guerrilla, thus further alienating public opinion. So far as I can see, guerrilla warfare on the scale employed in Zimbabwe was only possible because the people of the land offered a friendly or at least neutral environment. If they had strongly supported the government and were hostile to the guerrilla presence, informers would have done a brisk trade and the underground fighters swiftly identified and rooted out. If a government cannot count on the people's support, it is soon involved in a whole battery of repressive legislation to coerce the public into doing by law what they will not do willingly – create a hostile environment for the guerrillas.

Thus, Rhodesia's whole system of rigorous laws such as The Emergency Powers Act whose scope was self-evident, the 1975 Indemnity and Compensation Act, described by the former Federal Chief Justice, Sir Robert Tredgold, as a 'profoundly shocking act' and the Special Courts Regulations all announced to the world that the Rhodesian Government was at war not just with Patriotic Front guerrillas but also with the people of Zimbabwe. And it is clear that the Smith Government soon realized it. The then Minister of Defence, Mr P. K. Van der Byl said in the

Rhodesian Parliament, 'I have no intention of doing anything about this (the deaths of a number of African civilians shot on their way home from work by troops). So far as I am concerned, the more curfew breakers that are shot the better, and the sooner it is realized everywhere the better'. And the Secretary for Law and Order urged police cadets passing out in Salisbury in July 1976 'not to be squeamish in departing from the niceties of established procedures which are appropriate for more normal times'.

These were not the voices of the leaders and protectors of the people, but of the people's enemies. The guerrillas' first aim had been achieved – to speed up deteriorating relations between a discredited government and a restless people.

The most important thing then which marks off guerrillas from terrorists is that they do not make war on the people. They fight from amongst the people, primarily attacking military targets and goading an unpopular government into ever greater unpopularity. It is the security forces and not the guerrillas who end up making indiscriminate war – this is the lesson of many countries. In political terms, the battle is not between two armies nor between one army and an irregular force but between an army and the people. The immediate purpose of the guerrillas may be to harry the security forces but their long-term aim is to mobilize the people. The guerrilla war is a 'people's war' which is why the Viet Cong called their guerrilla forces – *Dan Quan* – 'civilian soldiers'. And the acid test of the justice of the conflict is the attitude of the people. If they are happy with their government the guerrillas cannot prevail in the long run: if they are not happy, then the guerrilla war will prove unwinable and it is only a matter of time before the government topples.

Guerrillas do not make war on the people. That is an inflexible rule not only for reasons of morality but because their survival depends upon keeping on good terms with the civilian population and especially with its natural leaders such as headmen, teachers, parsons and so on. This is why, leaving aside all questions of decency and fair play, it made no sense whatsoever for Patriotic Front guerrillas to murder missionaries. Guerrillas operating with difficulty in country heavily penetrated by security forces need every friend they can get and in Zimbabwe missionaries were, throughout the struggle, the only influential group of whites at all sympathetic to the guerrillas' cause. There is no logic in murdering your friends and at the same time creating a violent storm of world opinion against you.

It would be foolish of me to claim that no guerrillas ever behaved as terrorists in Zimbabwe or anywhere else; that they never took hostages or did acts of murder, rape and robbery. But here is a distinction worth making. They committed these crimes as citizens answerable to the normal codes of civilized behaviour, not under some special exemption offered to those serving as guerrillas. By the same token, members of the security forces who committed crimes against humanity could not plead special circumstances. The mini-morality at work within the general immorality of war applies. There is a distinction, obvious to any sane man or woman, between murder and causing death in the course of war.

There is no point in playing down the moral difficulties which arise in the course of even the most disciplined guerrilla campaign. Guerrillas can only merge with the general population by breaching that longstanding convention of war that soldiers and civilians should be quite clearly distinguishable in order that the innocent onlooker will not get hurt by mistake.

In modern wars, the difference between soldiers and civilians has shrunk almost to nothing, and deliberate decisions by statesmen and generals to destroy whole cities, the vast majority of whose inhabitants were noncombatants, have blurred all the old moral distinctions. Nevertheless, we must in the middle of madness cling to a little sanity. There are those who are properly targets of violence and those who are not, and guerrilla operations are bound to create some moral confusion. Presumably, civilians *are* civilians because they have this right of immunity from hostile activity, and it is because they have this immunity that guerrillas hide amongst them.

Security forces who respect the rights of civilians will put themselves at some disadvantage in this kind of war; those forces which do not respect these rights will commit widespread atrocities. This is the way the war in Zimbabwe progressed, or rather deteriorated, into a struggle which drew in more and more of the civilian population. We can take no refuge from responsibility in any naive claim that all guerrillas were saints and every government soldier was a devil. We are back to the margins of morality again, those mere percentages of evil which separate one side from the other.

We must remember that the guerrilla struggle was forced upon the people of Zimbabwe. The members of the Patriotic Front were not born as freedom fighters. It is a terrible trade they had to learn through sheer desperation, and I know of no evidence to suggest that with inevitable exceptions – the wicked minority for whom war provides unique opportunity for doing evil – guerrilla soldiers degenerated into terrorists.

Some lawyers would argue that there is a very fine line, if any at all, to be drawn between guerrillas and terrorists, because both groups operate by stealth and strike at random. I myself believe that there is a very important distinction which we ought not to let go of lightly. The aim of the terrorist is to strike fear into the people by killing indiscriminately. How is he to know who will be walking past the car in which he has planted a ticking bomb at the instant it explodes? He neither knows nor cares. The people must be demoralized, so anyone will do as a target. The guerrilla's goal is the precise opposite, not to break down the people but to build up their defiance, not to inspire fear but courage in them, not to carry the war to them but to carry them willingly into the struggle.

Terrorism demands no self-restraint, no honour, none of the qualities we prize in human beings. The guerrilla soldier calls upon resources of courage and discipline and sacrifice – qualities needed not only to achieve the revolution through war but to consolidate it in peace thereafter. The terrorist, on the other hand, is the enemy of true revolution, because the necessary qualities of his task are of no value once the phase of armed struggle is over. No one must be allowed to blur this distinction for the purposes of propaganda.

Zimbabwe – the Debate about Violence

When I began this essay – indeed, when I finished the last chapter – the shooting war in Zimbabwe was at its height.

157

Now it is over, thank God, and the people of that unhappy land can take charge of their own destiny for the first time this century. As for Zambia, she has lived with this tragic problem for as long as she has been an independent state. She was truly a war baby, born to the sound of gunfire on her northern, western and eastern frontiers; in the months prior to our Independence celebrations, guerrillas were already operating in Angola and Mozambique and the civil war in the Katanga spilled over from time to time into our Minilungu District. And across the Zambezi, the determined preparations of the white minority regime to resist to the limit even the broken-backed efforts of Britain to get a square deal for the Africans of Zimbabwe were apparent to all observers other than those who saw the world through the windows of Whitehall clubs.

Zambia has paid a very heavy price for British weakness. Our economy has been crippled from the side-swipe of sanctions and the proud development plans we evolved to chart a bright future have had to be shelved or abandoned. Our population has been swollen by pathetic armies of refugees who, I regret to say, have not been safe from harm even within our borders because Rhodesia Air Force bombers made refugee camps a prime target – as though the poor souls had not suffered enough! And our hope of building Zambian society as an experiment in non-racism was seriously set back by the strong reaction of our people to the white racists in the South – more than once I had to warn black Zambians after flare-ups in Livingstone and the Copperbelt against 'seeing a Smith in every white face'. As for our foreign policy, it has become so distorted by the Zimbabwe affair that we have scarcely been able to lift our eyes beyond the Zambezi and discover our true role in world affairs. For Zambia has, I truly believe, a destiny far wider than that of being the main opponent of white racist regimes in Southern Africa.

I have sworn a vow to resist the temptation of reminding the British Government in the past few weeks, 'I told you so!', though I do not know whether to be amused or annoyed by their present air of self-congratulation on achieving what they spent most of the post-war years trying to prevent or at least hold back – the end of white domination in Zimbabwe. But this is no time for trying to score debating points – it is the prospect of a just peace in Zimbabwe that matters: let history award the prizes.

It is much too early to conduct a postmortem on the Rhodesian tragedy; there are mountains of documents to sift and the sun to set many times on our long-accumulated anger before we can see the truth with unclouded eyes. My present purpose is to offer some comments on the question of the use of force in Zimbabwe. It is one thing to discuss violence as a philosophical issue, quite another to come to terms with it as a practical option in a specific case. The best starting point is to ask an obvious question: why, if it was possible to hold free elections leading to majority rule in Zimbabwe in 1980 was it not possible to do the same around the time in 1964 when the other two partners in the defunct Federation, Zambia and Malawi, became independent? The simple answer is that in 1964 the Rhodesian settlers were still so confident in their power to handle any unruly blacks that they would have resisted the British Government fiercely even had the imperial power the will or inclination to impose majority rule. And of course if a lion lies on its back waving its paws in the air you are not disposed to take its growls too seriously.

In 1964 there was not the slightest evidence of organized militancy amongst the black population of Rhodesia; nothing to cause those who controlled a highly efficient army, air force and paramilitary police to lose any sleep. The chosen leaders of the African people were in and out of gaol or detention so frequently that they had little opportunity to organize their followers or plan any grand strategy. And the Government skilfully perpetuated traditional tribal divisions, undermining black solidarity by appointing chiefs who were paid lackeys – men of straw. Just over a decade later, not one but two highly disciplined and efficient guerrilla movements had fought the Rhodesian forces to a standstill, convincing all but the most die-hard white settlers that their cause was lost. The effect of sanctions was minimal as was the flurry of British diplomatic activity – Prime Ministers taking Mr Smith for two cruises around the Mediterranean in HMS *Tiger* and HMS *Fearless*, the talks about talks, the emissaries and commissioners flying busily in and out of Salisbury – much noise, activity and little more. On my farm, I have noted that it is the hens which cluck the loudest and raise most dust that lay the fewest eggs. Meanwhile, the Africans of Zimbabwe, seeing clearly that there was no one else around with the will to save them, got on with the ghastly business of fighting, bleeding and dying.

This contrast between the degree of militancy of the Zimbabwe nationalists in 1979 and 1964 is a factor of the utmost importance because it demonstrates that the armed conflict in Zimbabwe was a classical anti-colonialist war, a freedom struggle in which an oppressed people were driven through desperation to take up weapons and had to learn the arts of war from scratch. The soldiers of the Patriotic

Front, whatever the propaganda machines in Salisbury and Pretoria said, were not an advance column of international communism moving in to take over Southern Africa; they were peasants and politicians, teachers and school children forced to take extreme measures by a combination of oppressive white racism and British betrayal. They started out as total strangers to the dark world of organized violence, and their earliest efforts were heart-rendingly pathetic. Armed with little more than a true love for their country, a burning indignation at the plight of their fellow Zimbabweans and the crudest weapons they marched to their doom at the hands of highly trained, well-equipped professional soldiers. They had no agreed strategy, knew nothing about tactics, did not even possess uniforms in the early days.

So Sir Harold Wilson's decision to rule out the limited use of force against Rhodesia in favour of a diplomatic and economic campaign is revealed to have been completely mistaken – Professor Robert C. Good, a former US Ambassador to Zambia and an eminent political scientist, has described it as 'a missed opportunity of historically great significance'. God knows, the decision to go to war is the most terrible a statesman must make, and he deserves to be, judged, whoever he is, with the utmost magnanimity. But the record shows with terrible clarity that Sir Harold's refusal to use a limited degree of force produced just those spillover consequences of widespread violence he was so concerned to avoid. In place of a pre-emptive strike lasting a few weeks, Zimbabwe was condemned to years of civil war. Is this not a clear example of the pacifist dilemma – that there are some circumstances in which a sincere desire to pursue the strategies of peace can condemn others to go to war in our stead?

My argument with the British Government about the use of force in Rhodesia is a fascinating and depressing example of the strange twists the complex debate about violence can take. Here was I, in 1965, a pacifist President trying to persuade Sir Harold Wilson to risk a minimal amount of violence by establishing a British military presence in Rhodesia, whilst he, certainly no pacifist so far as I am aware, was insisting to me and announcing to the whole world that under no conditions would he run the risk of war by sanctioning the use of even a token force. That one burst of pacifist zeal gave Mr Smith the green light to go ahead with UDI, assured both South Africa and Portugal they could interfere in Rhodesia's affairs with impunity and effectively neutralized in advance any organized opposition within Rhodesia to UDI – for what would be the point of demonstrating loyalty to the Crown if the only support Britain was prepared to offer you was rhetorical?

This is not the place to set out in detail my dealings with the British Government in this tragic matter. I merely want to sketch as honestly as I am able the evolution of my own attitudes to armed struggle in Zimbabwe. My ideas did not develop in a vacuum; they were shaped by dialogue and dispute with the other chief actors in this drama.

It was in 1963, before I had even been appointed President of Zambia, when I was still a Minister of a country on the eve of independence, that I had my first dispute with Britain over the disposition of armed forces. A central African Conference was held at the Victoria Falls to discuss the details of the break up of the Federation. One key question was that of the disposal of the Royal Rhodesia Air

Force, the most powerful air strike force south of the Sahara and north of the Limpopo. I argued strongly that at least half these aircraft should revert to Zambia because our copper revenues had largely paid for the lot. Britain was adamant that Rhodesia should have them. The reasons given are now academic but were something to the effect that the RRAF was a Rhodesian force manned by Rhodesians and based in Rhodesia and anyway Zambia did not have an airfield equipped to cope with jet fighters. Anyone flying in or out of Lusaka International Airport today must shake his head with disbelief. But these were the arguments. In retrospect, possibly I should have pushed harder but I was offered cash for development by way of compensation and my feeling was that resources to feed our people were very much better than the means to destroy someone else's people.

I lost the aircraft, I never got my development funds, and to rub salt in the wound, the next time I caught sight of those planes they were bombing Zambia's capital. If as the historians say, Britain's first calamitous mistake on the road to UDI was the decision in 1923 to grant Southern Rhodesia full control of defence matters – in effect, giving a white minority government the legal right to raise and control its own army – the second equally calamitous mistake was to hand over to Mr Smith that air force intact. Or was it a mistake? If you are really determined to establish representative government in one of your colonies do you offer on a plate a fiercesome weapon to the entrenched minority who have made it plain they intend to resist your actions to the death?

I was not as experienced then in the ways of the British as I am now, and my idealism, then untried, led me to think the best of my fellow men, however curious or even sinister were some of their actions. In the spirit of Gandhi my teacher, I went forward in openness and friendship to meet and embrace all those who had been our enemies in the freedom struggle, confident that love would evoke love and the spirit of forgiveness heal old wounds. I am not now ashamed of what some of my critics at the time called my naivety and lack of worldly wisdom. It is better to start off as an idealist, expecting the best from people even if occasionally let down, than to start off a cynic, always expecting the worst from people and always getting it.

I know this – I believe my country has been betrayed and tricked and misrepresented so much during the UDI conflict that had I not had a reservoir of idealism on which to draw when the going was toughest I would by now be so bitter as to be in danger of losing my very soul let alone my fitness to be a national leader.

It was partly to throw off the moods of despair which from time to time threatened to destroy me that I prayed and thought my way through to what has been somewhat grandly called the philosophy of Zambian Humanism. It is quite simply the good news about man derived from my study of the Bible and other great writings, supplemented by my own experience. It is intended to be an antidote to corrosive cynicism, a tonic for drooping spirits – those appalled by the dark side of human nature.

It is commonly assumed that those in public life who confess to a streak of idealism in their nature can be written off as politically soft-centred. In fact, the politicians who proved to be soft-centred about UDI were those who cast around frantically for some 'nice' alternative to the 'nasty' reality of irresistible nationalism. We are told that Sir

Harold Wilson refused to use force and threw away his strongest bargaining card by announcing his intentions publicly because he did not want to drive white Rhodesian moderates into the extremist camp. Now, I am not quite sure what the terms 'moderate' and 'extremist' mean in this context. Sir Harold in his memoir, *The Labour Government 1964-1970*, seems to count Mr Ian Smith amongst the 'moderates' whose sympathies were not to be alienated. In which case, who on earth were the 'extremists'?

One minor theme in the history of the freedom struggle in Africa has been the colonialist's search for 'moderates' who might be able to provide a 'nice' substitute for nationalism. By definition, the 'moderate', whether black or white, was less radical in his demands, more amenable to the voice of reason transmitted from Whitehall or wherever and usually shared the colonialist's values and attitudes – which made doing business with him a pleasure. So in Zambia in the years prior to independence we saw the rise and fall of a long succession of 'moderate' political parties, the Constitution Party, the Central Africa Party, the Liberal Party, all dedicated to goals such as 'multi-racialism', 'evolution not revolution' and 'partnership'. I must not be unkind about these short-lived movements, I had good friends in most of them and their hearts were in the right place but their political existence and hope of success was founded upon the illusion that black nationalism was simply a handful of extremist leaders stirring up trouble amongst the happy masses, and that moderation would prevail if only people like me were got out of the way either by conversion or incarceration. They collapsed, one after another, these parties, simply because people who are suffering great injustices are not 'moderate'. Their deep feelings issue in strong politics, and so they should. When there are serious conflicts of interest in any society, it is not moderation but futility to assume the problem will go away provided we sweet-talk those on both sides of the divide who feel least strongly.

One interesting thing about these so-called moderate political parties was the number of white Christians to be found amongst the membership. Indeed, one of them, the Constitution Party, was known to the press as the Parsons' Party because a reporter attending its inaugural conference had found so many clerical gentlemen in the hall he thought he had strayed into the Synod of the Anglican Church by mistake. Why is this, I have often wondered? I should hate to think it is because Christians feel bound to adopt only middle-of-the-road attitudes to political issues. There are surely some things about which they ought to be extremist in the sense that Christ was extreme in his refusal to compromise with evil. Many Christians still seem to feel they ought to steer well clear of the dirty business of politics, but if a sense of civic duty impels them to show willing, then better get tied up with 'nice' parties such as the Constitution Party than 'nasty' ones like the nationalist movements.

That is a digression but it does have a direct bearing on the UDI issue because it throws a brief spotlight on Bishop Abel Muzorewa, surely one of the truly tragic figures of the whole sorry mess. I have little doubt that it was a genuine desire to be an agent of reconciliation that first led this man of God to throw his hat in the political ring. He wanted to be an honest broker between the political authorities and the nationalist leaders who were at the time either in prison or exile. He was that breed of 'moderate' whom much cleverer political manipulators seize upon and use as a stalking horse. Being much more acceptable to the white minority than the nationalist leaders, he was flattered, encouraged and given all kinds of support, not least from big business, which thought its interests would be better served under a Muzorewa government than any other black variety. Tragically, the bishop began to believe his own propaganda and found the carefully stage-managed mass rallies and contrived adulation highly congenial. He tasted power – and liked it. Alas, he stood for a political fiction; he represented nothing real in the Zimbabwe situation and when the people were given their first real chance to declare their will, he was humiliatingly defeated.

So another 'moderate' bit the dust. But the colonialists and those who share their predatory appetites will go on trying to undermine the freedom struggle by tricking well-meaning but not politically astute moderates into thinking there can be some middle way between justice and injustice, that it is worth tolerating a little slavery rather than a lot, and that repressive minority regimes will mend their ways if you talk nicely to them and wait patiently for them to grant the masses as a concession what is already theirs by God-given right. Men and women of peace, especially those who pacifism is based on religious convictions, are obvious targets for such propaganda because, like all sane human beings, they detest violence and will choose any course that has a chance of holding it off. Their motives are honourable, whereas the motives of the colonialists who recruit and use them are not so pure. It has been my experience in Southern Africa that when minorities in power make ringing appeals to moderates to join forces with them to prevent conflict what they are really doing is inviting moderates to help them stay in power a little longer.

I ended up supporting armed struggle in Zimbabwe because I could no longer believe that *anything* is preferable to the use of force. I have been much taken with some words of a Victorian writer, Douglas Jerrold: 'We love peace as we abhor pusillanimity; but not peace at any price. There is a peace more destructive of the manhood of living man than war is destructive of his body. Chains are worse than bayonets.' Yes, if one must make that terrible choice, I *do* believe that chains are worse than bayonets. We never had the luxury of choosing between the strategies of perfection and those of harsh realism. We never had any option but to weigh up one form of evil against another and ask for God's forgiveness as we undertook to do what had to be done. Or at least we did have one other option, and this is the final ironic twist to the saga of UDI. I still believe that had Britain been prepared to risk a limited degree of force at the outset she might have achieved a just peace. But for whatever reasons she chose the way of misguided pacifism and made years of civil war inevitable.

The Last Laager

Now there remains the most entrenched and powerful enemy of human rights in Southern Africa -- the Republic of South Africa. One quite crucial question is this. What lessons has Britain learned from the Zimbabwe conflict? Will the old colonial attitudes be buried as Rhodesia dies and Zimbabwe comes to birth or will they still haunt the corridors of Whitehall and Westminster? Will Britain continue to apply to South Africa all the old assumptions about white minorities and black majorities that were totally discredited in Rhodesia? Is there any hope that Britain may make one small act of restitution for her failure in Zimbabwe and give her policy towards Southern Africa not just a face-lift but a complete overhaul? Or are we fated to hear all the old nonsense trotted out about South African whites knowing what is best for the blacks – who are perfectly happy with their lot unless stirred up by the agents of international communism? Shall we continue to be told that the human rights of the black people can be bought for the price of tinkering with the notices at the entrances to hotels and sports grounds; that limited economic advancement will serve to take their minds off their political rights? Does Britain still believe that her long term economic interests are best served by backing the whites against the blacks in South Africa? Does the British Foreign Office with its centuries of diplomatic experience share the view of history held in Pretoria that the great flood tides of human liberation and advancement now sweeping across the world and down the African continent can be held back at the Limpopo indefinitely?

The answer in a rational world has got to be No, of course Britain does not believe such things! Then why does she continue to behave as though she did?

I know I shall be told that South Africa is a very different proposition from the old Rhodesia. Of course she is militarily more powerful – and it may be that there is truth in the rumours that she has produced and exploded a nuclear device in partnership with Israel. Of course she has immense economic strength, thanks to her wealth in precious metals and stategic ores. Of course the racial attitudes of the white minority have the force of religious fanaticism, some crazy perversion of Christianity. All these things are true, but surely the lesson of the freedom struggle in Zimbabwe is now plain to our black brothers and sisters in South Africa? Once captive peoples awake and become conscious that freedom is possible, that they are not a strange species denied what the rest of mankind enjoys, then the oppressor's days are numbered. And he is powerless, in the last resort, to prevent the inevitable, because he is trying to fight not an army but an idea, and short of exterminating a whole population he cannot bomb or blast it out of their minds.

South Africa's powerful military machine cannot save her because the crucial engagements will not be fought on any battlefield. There was no Armageddon in Rhodesia and I very much doubt there will be one in South Africa even though our Afrikaaner friends like to do things according to the Bible. To all intents and purposes, the minority regime will start to lose the war when ordinary white citizens are no longer able to enjoy their stay in paradise because they have lost for ever their sense of security. How did the whites in Rhodesia end up? Their homes were like armed fortresses and they could not go about their daily business without weapons at their hip. It was hazardous to walk down a city street and almost suicidal to drive in the country. It dawned on them they were at war not with a handful of guerrillas but a whole people when they could not look a black man or woman in the eye and be sure they were seeing a friend. Their national wealth, instead of providing a better life for all, was more and more eaten up by the war machine, and the lives of their young people were disrupted by conscription in order to fight a war they could not win even if it lasted for a thousand years. That was the first and decisive battle the Rhodesian whites lost – the destruction not of their army but of their peace of mind.

I dread the prospect of a similar fate overtaking the whites in South Africa though I fear that much of the apparatus of a police state at war is already in place. Far from banging some militarist drum and preaching the inevitability of violence, I continue to pray and work for any reconciliation with South Africa on the basis of justice for all her people. It is somewhat distasteful to list one's credentials but it seems pertinent to this present discussion to point out that I have taken considerable political and personal risks to try to keep some dialogue going with South Africa. The chances of persuading the minority regime to change its policies have always been poor but still worth persevering with until the very end.

As long ago as January 1964, on the eve of the elections which were to put UNIP in government and lead to my appointment as first Prime Minister of Northern Rhodesia, I addressed a press conference in Broken Hill (as it was then called). There I scandalized some of my comrades by offering, if we were elected to power, to exchange ambassadors with South Africa. My sole condition was that the staff of our mission should be given the same respect as that shown to diplomats from European countries: they must not be subjected to the indignities of *apartheid*. My reasons for making this offer were stated plainly in an interview I gave at the time to a journalist of the Johannesburg *Star* which reported me as saying, 'I find myself obsessed with the tremendous problem of South Africa. If bloodshed really does begin in South Africa, it would have a ghastly effect, not only within the Republic itself, but throughout the whole continent of Africa. I have searched my heart for a new approach to help all South Africans to solve their problem peacefully. In my opinion, the present is the most critical psychological moment to show there is understanding and sympathy for the people of South Africa'. So my present opinions have not been recently acquired. They are all of a piece with the deep convictions I have held about Southern Africa from the time I was first appointed to any government office.

I got no reply from Pretoria about my suggestion about exchanging ambassadors. Nor did I have better luck a few months later when I offered South Africa what amounted to a pact of mutual non-aggression. In June 1964, sentences of life imprisonment were passed on Nelson Mandela and seven other South African National Congress leaders. I sent a cable to President Swart asking that he commute their sentences to exile in Zambia, in return for which I would give him an assurance that we would not allow our country to be used as a base for subversive activity against the Republic. Again, only total silence from Pretoria.

It would be wearisome to set down all the diplomatic exchanges I have had with South Africa since that time. In any case, most are a matter of public record – Mr Vorster saw to that, when in 1971 he broke every convention of diplomatic confidentiality by publishing extracts from our personal correspondence, selected in a most tendentious way. I had nothing to hide so I reacted by making public all our correspondence relating to UDI in full. The London *Times* in an editorial headed, 'A Funny Way to Run a Dialogue' commented that Mr Vorster's action was 'an obvious diplomatic blunder'. Well, we all make mistakes, but Mr Vorster's problem is that he and his colleagues go on making the same mistake over and over again – which is to assume that all Africans are fools. I was well aware that South Africa's aim throughout the period of UDI was to split Zambia off from the rest of black Africa so that we would form one more layer of the cushion protecting the Republic from the psychological and military pressures of the rest of the continent. As long ago as 1968, the then Foreign Minister of the Republic, Dr Muller, gave the game away when he told *The Star*, 'The really valuable "conquest" and the one which would consolidate our defence bloc and make it almost impregnable would be Zambia. . . .'.

It seemed to me then, and it still does, that it is worth being misunderstood or even thought a fool if it is possible to avert all-out war at the southern tip of the continent. I know that some of my colleagues have been unhappy about these dealings with the 'Devil' and there are freedom fighters too, who think I have been sitting down and parleying with their great enemy. I understand their feelings – South Africa has so much to answer for at the bar of history. *Apartheid* is such a stinging slap in the face not only of black Africans but of all humanity that it is hard to be polite let alone talk seriously to those who practise it. But it must be done. Almost any price is worth paying to avoid the risk of Africa's ultimate war.

Almost any price – except one. We will never, never rest until Africa is wiped clean of the foul stain of *apartheid*. We cannot live with it, or come to any accommodation with those who impose it on the black masses of South Africa. On a number of occasions, from the time of the 1969 summit conference of East and Central African States onwards, we leaders of black Africa have tried to reassure the South African Government of our peaceful intentions. The manifesto issued after that conference stated, 'We would prefer to negotiate rather than destroy, to talk rather than to kill. We do not advocate violence; we advocate an end to violence against human dignity now being perpetrated by the oppressors of Africa'. We went on to assure white minorities that 'we believe that all the peoples who have made their homes in the countries of Southern Africa are Africans regardless of the colour of their skin, and we would oppose just as firmly a racist majority regime as a racist minority regime'. In other words, we take full account of South Africa's complex history and the presence there of white settlers who have no other homeland. So we have never demanded majority rule in South Africa tomorrow, but we insist that there should be universal human rights in South Africa today.

It is vital that Britain and the West take full account of the depth of our feelings about *apartheid*. It is not just a policy with which we disagree, nor is it some temporary social arrangement between the races that South Africa may be expected to outgrow in due time. No amount of playing around with integrated sport and other virtual irrelevancies can hide the unspeakable reality of what is not a political programme at all but possibly the most systematic attempt to rob a whole people of their humanity since the days of the Nazis' 'final solution' to the Jewish problem.

We can never remind ourselves too frequently just how blasphemous a creed *apartheid* really is. It seeks to do nothing less than obliterate the image of God in a large part of humanity. Firstly, it denies black people *the right to be*. It forces them to conform to an image which the Master Race has created of them – stereotypes symbolized by all those insulting and cruel names such as Nigger, Kaffir, Munt, Boy.

This philosophy of black inferiority is enshrined in South Africa's laws and customs and prevents the black people from being themselves – themselves not as whites see them but as God has made them. They are fixed, frozen, at a given point in time. There can be no development of personality, no room for either excellence or equality, no better tomorrow except on the basis of minor palliatives thrown down like bones before a dog – except that white South Africans love their dogs.

As in an enormous block of ice, the African people are held immobile. Whereas a white child has, in theory, limitless development, the potential for unfettered excellence, the black child can only be what his fathers were – better educated, higher paid, possibly, but still imprisoned within a system which hampers his movements, confines his energies and cripples his spirit. He can only *be* what a group of white men, playing God and holding political power at a particular point in history decree he must be. And this image, upon which exponents of *apartheid* base their government policies, systems of education and economic doctrines, their religion even, is made up of a collection of myths about the black man's past and fears about his future – myths which are the product not of sick minds but of diseased souls.

Secondly, *apartheid* denies its victims *the right to belong.* Through its policy of racial segregation, it imposes unnatural divisions on society, choosing a quite irrelevant standard, that of skin pigmentation, to fix the boundaries of community. The so-called doctrine of separate development creates a social monstrosity in just the same way that robbing a child of all contact with other human beings will turn him into some kind of human monster. Indeed, the

175

very name – separate development – is a contradiction in terms; it is morally indefensible, economically mad and politically explosive. It is morally indefensible because God created man in his own image and only the totality of human community can demonstrate the fullness of the divine image. It is economic lunacy because modern industrial and commercial systems depend not only on the maximum use of human resources but also on the application of these resources at the point of greatest effectiveness. Hence men and women who could enhance the economic performance of the nation are allowed to rot in reserves and Bantustans far distant from the places where they could make the maximum contribution to the nation's life.

And segregation is politically explosive because it implies an unequal distribution of resources and enshrines injustice. It gives the lion's share of what is going – wealth, land, education – to one group and keeps the other group in penury. By its gross deformity of the shape of true community it generates tensions which must sooner or later blow the nation apart because there is no way that genuine indignation and desire for justice can find a constitutional outlet. Segregation denies the richness and variety of the human heritage. It proposes the monotony of a garden filled with flowers of a single colour, the loneliness of a community made up of only one sex, the lack of attainment of organisms made up of a single cell.

Thirdly, *apartheid* denies its victims *the right to have*. The Charter of the United Nations Organisation lays down certain fundamental human rights which all persons possess for no other reason than the fact they are human. It is the willingness of a nation to grant these rights to every one of its citizens without regard to colour, class or ability which marks it off as civilized and fit to be a member of the international community. *Apartheid* reserves certain rights to a particular racial group – education, job possibilities, the power to vote, to have a share in government, even the right to worship God freely. Others have these rights either entirely withheld or granted only in limited degree – presumably because those in power do not regard them as fully human. Thus *apartheid* discriminates in favour of the strong, the privileged, the wealthy, whereas it is a widely accepted truth that the modern state must exercise its power to protect those who would otherwise go to the wall – the weak, the young, the old, the sick. Obviously, a truly egalitarian society is a dream until all its members can engage in healthy competition from a position of comparable opportunity. Every man, woman and child has a right to a place at the feast of life and the main policy drive of any enlightened nation must be to reduce those inequalities which rob human beings of their chances through no fault of their own.

Lest I be accused in all this of selective indignation about South Africa, let me make it clear that Zambia, though a loyal member of the Organisation of African Unity, has protested again and again that the OAU's silence on the tyrannical behaviour of some black states contrasts starkly with the stridency of her attacks on South Africa. We cannot with integrity call down the judgement of God on white tyrants in Africa and hold our peace whilst our brothers and sisters are slaughtered by black tyrants. Our public condemnation of black dictators such as Amin, Bokassa and Nguema was not popular in some quarters. We were accused of breaking ranks and giving comfort to the white minority regimes in Africa. Quite the contrary:

we have earned the moral right to speak about South Africa because we have attacked tyranny wherever we have come across it on the African continent. And I need no reminding that we must monitor constantly our own domestic policies and probe our deepest motives in case we end up condoning in Zambia what we condemn in the rest of Africa.

In sum, what is at stake in South Africa and also Namibia is simply man's right to be human – and that cannot be negotiable in return for supplies of uranium and precious metals, favourable terms of trade or even the chance to play against an excellent rugby team. *Apartheid*'s challenge not only to Africa but to all humanity is so absolute that if there is no other way we must face up, as the free world has done before in this century, to a long, hard struggle which cannot exclude the use of force. Pray God we may all be preserved from such an awful fate. Only South Africa herself has the power to avert what is rapidly becoming inevitable by demolishing the whole vicious apparatus of *apartheid*, setting all her peoples free from captivity to the past and offering her immense talents and energy in the service of the development of the whole continent. I am not optimistic, but I have much faith in the providence of God. That alone seems to stand between us and the void.

Postscript about Forgiveness

I do not feel I have got much nearer solving the riddle of violence nor of reconciling involvement in the use of force with my belief in the central importance of the cross. I live with this tension as a daily sadness, trying hard not to get too morbid nor spread gloom around my family and friends. At the same time I know that for me there is no way out of the dilemma by trying to rid myself of one half of the problem. To rule out the use of force under any circumstances in Namibia and South Africa might be to condemn millions of our brothers and sisters to indefinite servitude. That, surely, cannot be right. And yet, if it were not for that insistent inner voice (the ghost of a younger Kaunda?) arguing 'Surely, there must be some better way!' I could so easily tire of those apparently fruitless peace initiatives and settle for the inevitability of violence without further question or qualm. If we must even contemplate offering violence to our fellow human beings it is always better to do so against the pressure of an uneasy conscience. That way at least we do not get a taste for blood.

There is one antidote to despair to which I have been turning with great relief in recent days – I have been discovering or rather re-discovering the power of forgiveness. If I have found no way of coming to terms with the cross as a political strategy, at least I have been able to cling to it as a means of personal regeneration. The old hymn says it all in one line, 'He died that we might be forgiven . . .'. This is a deep Christian truth which accords well with the African temperament.

Being a long-time opponent of racism I ought not to boast about my own people, but if there is one thing the African people are supremely good at it is forgiving their enemies. Surely Zimbabwe is an obvious and topical example of this truth. Over thirty thousand Africans died in that utterly needless civil war and more than a million more were made homeless. Their leaders such as Robert Mugabe and Joshua Nkomo and many others were robbed of the best years of their lives in prison, detention and exile. The Rhodesian authorities even refused to allow Robert Mugabe to leave his prison cell to comfort his wife when their infant son died. Yet these are the same leaders who have gone to extraordinary lengths to assure whites that they have nothing to fear at the hands of their African fellow citizens in the new Zimbabwe.

There could be no better practical demonstration of the spirit of forgiveness than the sentiments expressed by Prime Minister Robert Mugabe, in a broadcast to the Zimbabwe nation on Independence Day, 17 April 1980. He said, 'If yesterday I fought with you as an enemy, today you have become a friend and ally in the same national interest. If yesterday you hated me, today you cannot avoid the love which binds you to me and me to you. It could never be a correct justification that because the whites oppressed us yesterday when they had power that the blacks must oppress them today because they have power. . . .'.

That says it all. Most of the African Frontline Presidents have stood where Mr Mugabe now stands, with the power but not the heart and will to wreak vengeance. I very much doubt we shall hear anything about Zimbabwe versions of the Nuremberg trials or war crimes tribunals. Yet it would be silly to imagine that decades of unnatural if not downright bad relations between the races can be reversed in a few months. Forgiveness is not an isolated act like the granting of a pardon, it is a constant willingness to live in a new day without looking back and ransacking the memory for occasions of bitterness and resentment.

Forgiveness is not, of course, a substitute for justice. Forgiveness is a free gift, not something we earn, but to know the reality of forgiveness we must be prepared to turn our backs on the things we have done which required us to seek forgiveness in the first place. One Christian friend asked me why South African blacks could not forgive the whites and so avoid a racial holocaust. I am puzzled that a Christian could even think that it is possible to have it both ways – receive forgiveness and still continue to commit the sin which requires that forgiveness. Justice and forgiveness are, I think, related this way. To claim forgiveness whilst perpetuating injustice is to live a fiction; to fight for justice without also being prepared to offer forgiveness is to render your struggle null and void. Justice is not only about what is due to a human being; it is also about establishing right relationships between human beings and this is impossible if our hearts are vengeful and bitter. We shall end up having to fight our wars all over again.

I have come to the conclusion that the willingness to forgive our enemies is not only a moral or religious matter; our very sanity might well depend upon it. For how at the end of the day can the guilty party make reparation for crimes so horrible that any compensation would be pathetically inadequate? What can those who master-minded or executed the plan to murder six million Jews put in the scales of justice to balance their crime? And what is the minimum the survivors of that horror might be prepared to accept as a just reparation? The whole world does not contain enough treasure to pay that bill. So unless we are able to forgive the enemies who cannot possibly make up to us for what they have done we go stark raving mad with bitterness and hatred.

I have seen the bodies of innocent refugees in Zambia blown to bits by Rhodesian bombers and my soul has been so tormented by my raging mind and angry heart that had I not been able to forgive my enemies because Christ has forgiven me, I should have become deranged with fury. And what is worse, any new relationship with the Rhodesian whites who did these things would have been utterly impossible. And that must be a double tragedy – for the state of my soul and for the relations between Zambia and Zimbabwe. Africa cannot afford the luxury of such feuds.

History, or rather colonialism, has imposed upon Africa the repeated shock of sudden ends and amazing new beginnings. Compare a map of the continent today with 1958 when Ghana was the only free nation in black Africa. Now there are independent states all over the map and none of them came into existence by a gradual process of evolution – the dispossession of the colonial powers was, according to the timescale of a continent a sudden and shocking thing. In less then twenty five years three centuries of European overlordship came to an end. This meant that the power relationships between races and tribes and regional groups were upset. And so deep, historically, had these divisions been that were it not for the spiritual strength of the African character, which shows itself in a willingness to let byegones be byegones, the entire continent would have been engulfed by the flames of war. Certainly, some of our Western critics point to contemporary trouble spots in Africa as evidence of the foolishness of allowing us to rule ourselves – not of course, that the colonial powers had any choice in the matter. I will not pause to argue, except to comment that it seems to me that compared with the wars and conflicts which accompanied the growth of Western Europe, Africa has been an oasis of calm.

It is by the power of forgiveness we are freed from the burden of past guilt so that we can act boldly in the present.

I think of some of Zambia's whites who were amongst my bitterest enemies during the freedom struggle. They have since concluded that they were mistaken, which makes me very happy, but they *will* keep harping back to those days, wringing their hands and repeatedly expressing regret. I try to say to them that they just do not understand what forgiveness means. They have been offered forgiveness but refuse to accept it. All that matters now is that they should stand shoulder to shoulder with us in building up the nation. This is surely what forgiveness is about – the freedom to stop going back to our past mistakes and feeling the pain of them again?

Even as I rejoice about the power of forgiveness and boast of the African's great capacity for it, I must be on my guard against putting myself and my comrades amongst those who, according to Jesus, 'trusted in themselves that they were righteous, and despised others'. It is only a short journey from the company of the forgiven to the ranks of the self-righteous. Even to talk of forgiving my white enemy can become pious cant unless we remember always that the most important thing about us both is that God loves us equally and finds the moral difference between us insignificant. I think it is safest only to take pride in those things which reflect no credit on us personally. I am proud of my country, very proud indeed of my family – I can take only a tiny bit of credit for either – but to take pride in the African capacity for forgiveness is a very dangerous thing indeed unless we remember that its source is in the divine mercy and not in our own spritual qualities.

I do not know how, in the context of political and social life, we can forgive as absolutely as Christ demands when he says, 'Let him that is without sin cast the first stone'.

183

The foundations of law and order would collapse through an acute shortage of sinless policemen and perfect judges, and the conduct of international affairs would be impossible. Does our inability to attain such absolute standards mean we must resign ourselves to the fact that until the earth is transformed in the Kingdom of God, we have just got to behave as honourably as we can in the midst of conflict and hold the spirit of forgiveness in reserve until hostilities have ceased?

My conclusion is that though I and my enemy cannot always, in the absence of justice, reach a point of agreement which makes conflict unnecessary, there *is* a perspective from which 'all our righteousness is as filthy rags', our differences, however precious to us, insignificant, and the question of who wins quite irrelevant. It is this realization which should drive us even in the heat of conflict to seek God's forgiveness. My enemy and I have many differences, some of which have brought us to the point of conflict; the one thing we share is the need to be forgiven.